Youth
Considers
Parents as People

YOUTH FORUM SERIES

Titles in Print

Youth Asks, Why Bother About God?
  by Alvin N. Rogness
Youth Considers Sex
  by William E. Hulme
Youth Considers "Do-It-Yourself" Religion
  by Martin E. Marty
Youth Considers Parents as People
  by Randolph Crump Miller

Titles in Preparation

Youth Considers the World of High School
  by John S. Wood
Youth Considers Life Goals
  by Ross Snyder
Youth Considers Personal Moods
  by Reuel L. Howe
Youth Considers Doubt and Frustration
  by Paul L. Holmer

YOUTH FORUM SERIES

Youth
Considers
PARENTS AS PEOPLE

by

Randolph Crump Miller

THOMAS NELSON & SONS

London   NEW YORK   Toronto

Second Printing, November 1966

© 1965 by Randolph Crump Miller

Library of Congress Catalog Card Number: 65-22013

Printed in the United States of America

TO

CAROL

Foreword

Written in the context of the Christian faith, this book is one in a series published by Thomas Nelson & Sons in collaboration with Church Youth Research.

The research agency, which serves as editor of this series, is known through *What Youth Are Thinking* (Smedsrud, 1961) and *Profiles of Church Youth* (Strommen, 1963). The Director, Dr. Merton Strommen, is known also for his work as Director of Research (1965-67) with Religious Education Association, an inter-faith agency serving all church groups.

The purpose of the series is to use points of established need to bring about meaningful contact between the GOSPEL of God in Jesus Christ and YOUNG PEOPLE. Underlying the total effort is a concern that youth throughout the English-speaking world can be helped to see that the Gospel of Christ is the core of life itself in all its realities.

Unique to this publication effort is the use that is made of research findings. These describe the specific need to which each book is addressed as well as the youth most concerned about this need. Thus a writer is helped to speak more directly to the actual conflicts, values, and beliefs of an important segment of youth.

The significance of this series is enhanced by the scholarship and pastoral concern of the authors. Their grasp of the fields in which each writes enables them to speak with authority, establishing the series as a basic reference in the area of youth work.

Preface

Our bookshelves are full of books written to help parents understand teenagers, their own or others. Now here comes a book written to serve the reverse need—to help teenagers understand adults and parents, their own or those of other young people.

This attempt has not been made very often and there are not many writers as audacious as Randolph Crump Miller to throw themselves willingly into such a dangerous endeavor.

In my judgment, he brings it off wonderfully well. This appraisal is, of course, a biased judgment, for I, too, am a clergyman, a parent, about the age of the writer, and, in general, one who shares in his outlook on life and in his theological stance.

"Theological stance?" you may ask. Yes, there is one here; indeed, it would not have been possible to avoid such a position. For when one begins to talk about authority, about rebellion and independence, about moral values, and about the marks of a Christian, one is involved in theology, implicit or openly formulated. Professor Miller's theology grows out of life and returns into life situations to make them more meaningful and rich.

Communication across the barrier of age-differences is not easy at best. Young people have not had the experiences of adults. There is a perennial inability of young people to believe that parents were ever youthful in mind and spirit. There is an almost universal tendency of parents to forget or at least to distort, always for the better, their own earlier years. And so it is that sons and daughters come to be strangers to their parents, and parents to them. Not until marriage and parenthood come along to young people, in turn, does common ground reappear, reclaimed from the estrangement of perhaps a decade.

Dr. Miller's book will help this common understanding come about at an earlier stage in life than marriage or parenthood. If it is thoughtfully read and reread this common understanding will be broader and deeper than it otherwise could have been.

Professor Miller has spent most of his life as a minister and teacher. I have spent most of mine as a minister and educational administrator. My work has brought me into close contact with leaders in the educational work of the churches in every part of this country. In a superficial way I have come to know something of the problems of Christian teachers, parents, young people, and church leaders in three other continents. All over the world there is found this lack of common understanding, this lack of "meeting." In every nation I've seen and in every national church situation I've come to know, this book will be helpful.

Not equally so in all places, of course. Nor will all the author says apply everywhere. The descriptions he draws for us, however, are to be found nearly everywhere. The counsel he gives reaches across national and continental boundaries. Tokyo and Teheran, as well as Terre Haute, will find it useful.

My own work brings me in contact with young people frequently enough to hear the observation—not quite a complaint but almost that—"Well, these are not easy times in which to grow up." They aren't. How we adults wish they might be better for young people!

Our times are not, by the same token, easy times for adults and parents. They are, however, the only times we have and we shall live in them wisely and well to the extent that parents and young people understand each other and live together with insight, understanding, and acceptance.

I have only one regret about this book. I wish I might have read it in the middle 1920's. It would have helped me, then a youth, to understand two fine people, my own Mother and Dad.

Gerald E. Knoff

National Council of Churches
Division of Christian Education

Contents

Introduction

This book is an attempt to give you an understanding, from a Christian point of view, of parental authority. It helps you to look at your parents, to see what they go through and why they behave toward you as they do, to see how their authority is established, and to come to grips with an understanding of your roles as young people and their roles as parents.

The book is written from a definite perspective, and you should be informed about it. In the first place, the issues that are discussed come from Church Youth Research, a long-term study of what young people really think about their parents and about the problems that are involved. So young people like you suggested the topics to be discussed. Parental authority is not the most important problem you have, for many of you live with and rely on it for guidance, though it gets under your skin from time to time.

In the second place, the perspective is that of a Christian view of life. It is natural, in a book like this, to refer to life in the church, where most of you spend some of your time; to the Bible, which most of you have read; and to a view of life in the world from a Christian standpoint.

In the third place, the book is written by a father of six children who is now a grandfather. He is widely acquainted with the issues that have plagued his children, the youngest of whom will be nineteen when this book is published, during their teen-age period. So you may think that the parents get the best of it in some of the things that are said in the following pages. You should be warned that the author is also a clergyman and a teacher in a seminary. So he brings in some Christian ideas to explain certain points.

But all through the book, he has kept you in mind. He is not defending the position of parents. Being one, he knows that no parent is perfect, that none can avoid grievous mistakes, and that all can misuse authority. But he also knows that his children can forgive him and love him in spite of his boners. And, strangely, he can still remember his relationship with his own father, which makes him sympathetic to you with some of your problems.

The theme of the book is simple: Keep open the channels of communication. Seeing that you have the parents you have, the best thing you can do is to enter into dialogue with them, so that they will know what makes the wheels go around in you and you will find out how and why they act as they do. If you can work at this, many of the other problems faced in this book can be worked out to your mutual satisfaction.

Randolph Crump Miller

the age group characteristics of parents between the ages of 35 and 50

This book is supposed to help you understand your parents and their authority. Because you are under their authority, at least legally, until you "come of age," you sometimes think of their authority as a basis of security, sometimes as a rope which relaxes slightly as you grow older, and sometimes as something to be dreaded and opposed at every possible point.

Before you can hope to untangle the problems posed by their use of authority, however, it might be helpful if you get an overall view of what parents are like. They have been studying you in terms of age group characteristics; they have read books on what makes adolescents do what they do and avoid what they avoid. So far as I know, no one has written a book about the age group characteristics of parents. So I propose that we observe the developmental stages of parents, looking primarily at their characteristics when they are between thirty-five and fifty, the age when they are most likely to have adolescent children.

YOUR EARLY YEARS

To start with, we have to go back to your beginning. When you were born, they were excited. They felt pretty cocky about the whole thing.

15

"Gee whiz," says a father, "*I* produced this!"

For the first three years, which you fortunately do not remember, you treated your parents as if they were gods. You were a helpless little baby, and when you yelled or cried they came as they saw fit. You were completely dependent on them. In them you lived and moved and had your being. You were fed when they thought you ought to be fed, you were put to bed when they wanted you to go to bed, and after awhile they decided to train you. They took you off the breast or the bottle and placed a cup against your lips, and you drank or starved. They took you out of dirty diapers and put you on a pot and waited for you to perform. They had absolute control over you. You rebelled sometimes by shouting or pushing the food away or by sitting and doing nothing, but you recognized their power. They had the power of life and death, just as God has.

Now this was very hard on parents. Being human, they were not used to being treated as gods, but when they got used to the idea, they liked it. And then what happened? You began to do things they could not control. You learned to climb out of the playpen even before you learned to walk; you had to be watched because they could not trust you. Maybe you landed on your head, so your mother put you back in the playpen and you did not climb out again for another week. But your world was expanding, and your mother had to be careful that you did not fall down the cellar stairs, or electrocute yourself on a floor plug.

NO LONGER A GODDESS

So your mother stopped being a goddess and started being a watchdog with a lively young animal to control. But she was proud that you could walk, and even more proud that you could talk. If you happened to say "Mama" as your first word, you built her ego up almost to goddess proportions again. Then, if you were smart, you tried on "Dada" for size and completely captivated him (especially if you are a girl). So in spite of running away and talking back, which you quickly learned as an assertion of your own individuality, you really had your parents spoiled completely by the time you were old enough to go to school. They were the authority figures, the absolute powers, and the source of all truth.

You did not realize what had been happening, of course, because it was the first time you had been through this stage and, if you were the first child, this was also the first experience for your parents. And they were not ready for what happened next. You went to school. You discovered that other children have parents. You found out that your friend's parents were different from your parents, and in some ways your friend's parents seemed to be better (maybe they gave you candy). But you still believed in the superiority of your parents, and when you were about seven you probably said to your friend, "My daddy can beat up your daddy."

Your friend became important in your life. When you cut your finger you asked your friend to bandage it instead of running to mother. You played with your friends and on a summer's day forgot to come home on time for dinner. In the old days you had been there and mother had plunked the food in your mouth. All of a sudden you were not even there; you were out playing baseball. And when you decided to come home to eat, you chose what food you would eat and what you would leave on your plate (if you could get away with it).

CUTTING YOUR PARENTS DOWN TO SIZE

You see what was happening to your parents. They were beginning to be cut down to size. You saw them as human beings with serious limitations. You may have said, without trying to be nasty although you succeeded, "Ma, why can't you be like Billy's mother? She's nice." This was rough on your parents. Some parents cannot take it, and try to keep their children as babies; such parents do not develop at all. So their children remain "mama's boys" or "daddy's girls" unless they begin to rebel right now. You began to say. "I want what I want, not what you want for me."

You probably found new chums and joined various clubs and found things to do outside of your home. You still had problems at home, though. You argued with your parents when they told you to turn off the TV. You said, "I don't want to go to bed," but daddy was still bigger than you, and you went. You did not rebel too much, and on the whole you got along pretty well. But your parents felt that their authority was shrinking, and pretty soon they would lose their darling child.

Then, after a period of relative quiet, came the explosion. You suddenly realized how dumb they were. You were convinced that you were smarter than they, and sometimes you thought you were smarter than your teacher. But your teacher knew more than your parents. Perhaps you had an intelligent teacher who told you about modern physics, nuclear fission, the space program, or even how an automobile works, and you mentioned this to your father and he began to tell you what he thought. You said, "No, Dad, you're wrong. My teacher told me what is so." You deflated whatever ego he had left, just like a punctured balloon. Long ago he had ceased to be a god in your eyes, and now he was not even an authority on what you were learning in the seventh grade.

If you are a boy, your father suddenly realized that you were no longer a child. You were shooting up, borrowing his razor, your voice was beginning to boom after you quit the boys' choir, and he realized that he could not put you in bed by physical strength any more. As one father put it, "The battle changed from physical to psychological warfare." Some fathers cannot make this shift and are left helpless.

If you are a girl, something similar happened. It probably dazzled your father when he discovered that he had a young lady on his hands, and he ceased to be a roaring lion and became like putty in your hands, at least some of the time. But he recovered. Your mother also was amazed at these sudden changes, not only because of what it told her about you, but because of the new kinds of demands and responsibilities that were placed on her as you began to face the problems of dating, making your own decisions, and, occasionally, asking her for advice.

So you started to cut your parents down to size, and in your own mind you cut them down *below* size. They were a nuisance because they got in the way of your freedom. You were trying to stand on your own feet and spent part of the time stomping on their toes. And your next question was, "When can I drive the automobile?" Just a short time ago you were a little baby, and now you want to take away the old man's automobile. Your father had to shift gears in more ways than one to adapt himself to this.

Most parents try to adjust. They read books. They consult with teachers and experts. They expect you to act your age. This causes more difficulty. They are uncertain concerning the amount of freedom *you* should have, for no two people are alike. Furthermore, one day you act as if you are fourteen, the next day you take responsibility as if you were eighteen, and then you simmer down to your actual sixteen. This gets very complex and it is no wonder that the parents are confused (as are you).

A LARGE FAMILY

It is more complex in a big family. Here is a girl in her mid-teens who is making her own decisions about dates, but she has a brother who is nine and is just beginning to compare his parents with other parents, and they have a younger sister who is three and who makes their parents feel like gods again. These parents have to be able to move from having absolute authority to competing with the fourth-grade teacher to accepting the freedom suitable to a young lady—back and forth, back and forth all day long.

Sometimes parents are smart enough to handle such complex situations as having a large number of children. When a boy is in the fifth grade, he measures everything by whether it is fair. He is always saying, "It isn't fair!" One boy wanted a fielder's glove which cost $5. His father agreed that it would be nice, but that because there were five brothers and sisters who would each have to have something else costing $5 the total would be $30. And daddy did not have $30. Because the boy was operating in terms of equal justice, he saw the point and agreed with it.

FAMILY RULES

Every family has to operate according to the rules of the game. Each family has a different set of rules. You probably have chores, such as washing dishes, mowing the lawn, taking out the rubbish, and so on. You do these things because you are part of a family. There are rules about meals, using postage stamps, paying for long-distance phone calls, buying gas for the car; such rules are set so that family life can run smoothly, but no two families have the same rules.

In one family, a junior high boy was limited to two bowls of cereal when he came in at five o'clock, because a third bowl would spoil his appetite for supper an hour later. But his sisters were limited to one bowl, because a second bowl would ruin their appetites.

Some parents are able to be consistent and flexible at the same time, providing the support of rules which a family needs and yet changing these rules as their children develop their capacities for greater freedom and responsibilty

PARENTS' ROLES

Another problem that besets parents is an understanding of their roles in today's world. Fifty years ago, the father was likely to be the authority and judge on most family matters. He was home often enough to make responsible decisions. If he were a farmer, he was right there. His store might have been next door to the homestead; he even came home for lunch.

Today's father is likely to be out of the house before the children have breakfast. If he is a commuter, he may return home after the children have had their dinner. He never sees his youngsters except when they are in bed, or if he gets home early he is so exhausted that mother "protects" him from the children. He does not have authority over anyone.

I once suggested to a group of young people that if they wanted their allowance in advance from their fathers, they should at least wait until after mother "had fed the beast" before approaching him. Their response was, "Why bother? We just ask our mothers." Father did not even have control of the money. He did not participate in the decision about allowances.

So a father is not sure of his role any more. He may think that his only value is that he makes the money which the family spends. He is "Mr. Moneybags" and not really a father.

Mother is equally confused. Is she supposed to be somewhat subservient to the father, as implied by the word "obey" which used to be in the marriage service? Is she supposed to consult with her husband before important decisions concerning the children are made? Sometimes your mother tries to be a wife, a mother, a worker in a club and the church, and to carry a job that makes money. She tries to be a mother and do all these things as well. Father works to make money, has some other outside activities, may go to church, and is around home only for a little while on weekends. So parents are both confused and filled with a sense of guilt. Their needs as *persons* are not being met by all the things that they are doing.

WHAT YOUR PARENTS NEED

Let us look at parents from another angle. If we are going to understand them, we need to see more clearly what their needs are. Above all else, they need exactly what you need: *to feel accepted and loved as they are.* Most parents do a good job of accepting and loving you as you are. They are able to forgive you for acts that they would not forgive in their neighbor's children. They frequently do not approve of what you do, but they love you just the same.

But how often are you able to show your parents that you love and accept them as they are? Particularly as you find out and expose their weaknesses when you become teenagers? You find it difficult to accept them when you are fighting against them. Sometimes you would like to kick them in the shins.

When the anger is past, you still love them. But most of you take your parents for granted. You do not bother to indicate your love, your forgiveness, your acceptance. Parents do make mistakes, and they try to cover them up with bluster rather than ask forgiveness. If you can keep open the channels of communication at this point, you can find some way to express your acceptance of them no matter what they have done.

The second thing that parents need is some kind of *regularity or structure* in their lives, just as you need rules to make life in the family run smoothly. It seems to some parents as if their children spent most of their time destroying the parents' schedule. Maybe your father likes to get his night's sleep, and you come home about an hour after he has gone to sleep and bang the front door and yell "Good night," and your friend "hot-rods" down the street in his car.

I remember this as a problem when I was young. My father was a clergyman. Saturday night was my favorite night for staying out late, but it was his favorite for going to bed early, for Sunday was a heavy day for him. I would come home from college in an old car with a tin can on the tail of a straight pipe exhaust, and the driveway went under the bedroom window. When I got in the house, I was sure of a "cheerful" greeting. I suppose it was not very thoughtful on my part, even though I came home from college after a date in order to teach Sunday school for him the next morning. I could have stayed at college and not taught that class. Or I could have given up my date with a blonde. But it never got to that point because we understood each other.

It is particularly hard on parents with a number of teenagers coming in at different times, so that the parents may be awakened at 11:30, 12:30, 1:30, and 2:00. You do not realize what this can do to parents who need their sleep, and who worry between arrivals. Two parents worked out an agreement with a sign-in sheet and no reports; the responsibility of the young people is to remain as quiet as possible. There is *agreement in advance about times for coming home,* but no check-up. The last one in turns out all the lights and locks up. This system worked very well until one Sunday morning it was discovered that the lights were on and one bed was empty. Sure enough, one girl was missing! Just after the discovery was made at 9 a.m., in she walked. The situation was perfectly innocent. They had been at a party at an engineering camp twelve miles off the highway. Due to a mix-up, the last car had left without them. They had to walk to the turnpike and then hitchhike home. The parents believed the story, and that was the end of it. But think what would have happened if the parents had begun checking about 4 a.m. They would have been reduced by worry to a state of anxiety long before their daughter arrived. Some parents cannot live securely in such a freewheeling situation, but others find such a solution helpful.

A third need of parents is *freedom to grow as persons.* Mothers have particularly difficult problems on this score. They can almost literally be locked in the house, even with all the modern conveniences. Washing, ironing, cooking, cleaning, and the companionship of babies do not always stimulate growth toward maturity. They seem to have a permanent baby-sitting job for about twenty years, and all the time they are dealing with children who are growing and changing in unpredictable ways. They cannot have mature conversations about politics, social problems, literature, philosophy, and religion, with babies and children. They do not have enough time with their husbands as wives and companions, because they are busy being mothers. They may be challenged and enriched by the joy of motherhood, and still feel frustrated. Even on vacations, many fathers stay on the job while mothers slave to keep the children happy.

Fathers have a different kind of problem. They grow in their jobs and have many outside interests, but under the pressures of modern life they do not have the opportunity to grow as fathers and husbands. I think that occasionally your parents should be free of their responsibility to you, so that they can enjoy their own companionship as husband and wife. They were husband and wife before you were born, and they will have a long time to live together after you have left home. One of your tasks is to help them find the freedom to grow together as persons.

PARENTS WORRY ABOUT YOU

Because your parents are concerned about you, they are likely to be filled with what seem to you to be unfounded worries. Your parents were young once, and they have vivid memories of the mistakes they or their friends made. Or they have read books which exaggerate the dangers of youth. This is particularly true in the area of sex. No matter how much your parents trust you, they know that sex is dangerous and that mistakes can occur. They have lived through this dangerous period, and you haven't yet. So they cannot be sure that you will be able to handle what seems to them to be dynamite. And the statistics show that there are plently of young people who cannot handle the problem adequately.

They have similar worries about your driving a car. They may recall some of their escapades at high speeds when they were young. They know the statistics of the insurance companies about boys under twenty-five. Yet you feel that the right to drive a car is the most important status symbol there is. Some parents are so fearful that they refuse to let their children apply for driving licenses at the legal age. Others would rather trust you to drive than some other young person. Some families have worked out rules. While you drive the family car, says one family, our agreement is that you will always stay within the speed limit. If you get arrested, you take the consequences and pay the fine or lose your license. If you have an accident, our insurance will cover you. Other families say, one arrest or one accident and you lose the right to drive.

One afternoon, Frank's father was teaching a class at the college. He called his father out and introduced him to a stranger. "Tell him, Dad," he said, "that we have insurance on our car and his." So his father assured the man that this was so. Then Frank explained that he had been driving home from school in his father's XKE Jaguar. It was snowing. Frank had the radio on, and in this state of warmth and pleasure he ran through a red light. The man's car struck the rear of the Jaguar, which wrecked the front end of his car and dented the rear fender of the Jaguar. Frank's father's only comment was, "You see, Frank, why our insurance rates went up when you started to drive." The car was in the shop for several days, and Frank kept asking when he could use the car. His father never reminded him who had put the car in the shop. Nothing more was said. Frank was allowed to drive again when the car was repaired, and he has never had another accident. He had learned the hard way. Other fathers might teach a similar lesson through anger, taking away the boy's license, or docking his allowance until the deductible cost is paid.

Parents worry about driving because it kills people. If their children are girls, they are more worried because girls ride in cars driven by others who may prove irresponsible. In one family there is an agreement that they will not ride with a boy who has been drinking; they will ask to drive or ride in someone else's car or phone home and ask their parent to come after them. This is a sane rule for saving lives.

Parents also worry about your choice of friends. They want you to be democratic, but sometimes they are surprised by the strange creatures you bring home. They know that you will be influenced by people you like and therefore they are concerned that you like people who will have a good influence. They do not want you riding with someone who has just stolen a car for a joyride. They are anxious about the gang you go with, because if the gang does anything wrong you will have to share the blame. They want you to be popular, but not at the expense of your integrity. And often you think they are suspicious of your friends or your gang when you think everything is all right.

Most parents also think it will be good for you if you go to Sunday school. Maybe your parents go to church, but even if they do not they probably think it is good for you to go. There may come a time when you are tired of what is taught in Sunday school and want to quit, and then you have a battle on your hands because they say you ought to continue. In some cases, you do not really want to quit, because everything is interesting, the teachers are effective, and your friends are there; but you react because you want to be free to choose. You are tired of being told you have to go. Yet you know, if you have really been exposed to the challenge of the Christian faith, that you never can know enough about Christian teachings or participate enough in Christian worship. But you do not like to have your parents harp on this all the time; and they are worried because you resent what they tell you.

Parents have another worry that sometimes annoys you. This centers on the problem of your education. They want you to be educated. They sometimes seem to want you to have more education than you can stand. So they put on the pressure, they use various forms of stimulus and bribery, they put in rules about homework, and they sometimes do everything they can to get you into college. What they often fail to understand is that all their children are not equally endowed with brains or incentive and that in a large family only two or three may be ready for college while the others will be happy if they complete high scool and take some technical training. Parents sometimes need help from the school authorities before they can understand what is best for you. Your parents may put on too much pressure or they may be too easy on you, and in either case it is not in your best interests. You need to be sympathetic with their efforts and seek to understand both their goals for you and your own aims in life.

PARENTS GROW OLDER

Parents get older, and as they do they tend to become more rigid. They like things the way they used to be. It is harder all the time to have the energy to roll with the blows and remain flexible as your enthusiasms bounce around and as your interests flame and die. Because you keep changing, moving back and forth between acting below and above your age, they do not always know where you are (and neither do you).

Your parents often seem out of date. They do not keep up with the latest dances or pop tunes. They like to play Dixieland music or they think that the latest pop tune is "Sweet Sue." New styles in eye make-up or hairdo come along, and all your father can say is, "Where is your face?" When they try to keep up with the latest jargon, you discover that they are about six months behind the latest "in" words.

As parents get older, they get tired more easily. Most of you recognize this and adapt to it. Some of you girls know that there is a certain time in the month when your mother is likely to be short-tempered. When your mother is somewhere around the age of forty-five to fifty, she goes through a certain change called menopause, and during this period of time her disposition may become less cheerful. Sometimes there is no observable change, but if there is, we should take account of it.

Then you need to remember that neither parent is worth much when they are having an argument. You are not able to do much about it, even as a peacemaker. After the argument, if they are still full of resentment, they may take it out on you, and if you do not understand why they are doing this you become blue, too.

The final thing to remember about parents during this period is that if they are normal sooner or later they want you to leave home. Like a mother bird, they toss you out of the nest so that you can fly on your own. Boys and girls are meant to leave home. If your parents are not willing to get rid of you, they are being possessive rather than showing love. Normal parents give you the freedom to leave when you are ready, and they stand ready to receive you back as an adult whenever you want to come back for a time.

For twenty to twenty-five years, your parents have spent most of their time concentrating on your welfare, and then comes the day when the last chick has flown from the roost.

Father looks across the breakfast table at mother and says, "Who are you and where did you come from?" This might happen if they were so busy being father and mother that they forgot to be husband and wife. So you need to help your parents remember that they are companions. A very wise wife and mother of seven put it this way:

"We the parents are lovers before we are parents. Our children are the fruit of our love as much as the fruit of our bodies. This is a fact of family life which we should never forget during those years when we concentrate on bringing up our children. Children are an incident in married life, a terribly important incident which needs all the attention and responsibility of which we are capable, but an incident no less. This is especially true today when families are small and the period of concentration is comparatively short for most couples. If our married life is a success, we will be lovers still when our work as parents is over." [1]

[1] *Background to Marriage,* by Anne Proctor, London: Longmans, Green and Co., 1953, p. 62. See *Your Child's Religion,* by Randolph C. Miller, Garden City: Doubleday & Co., 1962, pp. 149-150.

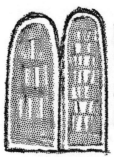

honor thy father and thy mother

John did not know how to tell the coach that he could not come out for football. He was big and strong and would almost surely make the team as a tackle. All he could do was tell the coach that he did not like football.

Actually, John loved to play football. During the summer he had worked out with his younger brothers. But his father had laid down the law. John was needed on the farm. Every morning before school there were cows to be milked, and after school they had to be milked again. So John came home on the earliest school bus and worked until dinner time.

The farm would not make money unless all the children worked. That was why there was a big family. And on the farm, his father was the boss. So there was not time for football or for social activities. Even on Sunday, chores had to be done before the family went to church.

And when John went to church, he heard the commandment, "Honor thy father and thy mother." How could he honor a man who was nothing but a slave driver, who thought of his children as slave labor, and who never gave them a chance to be themselves?

John could hardly wait until he was old enough to leave home, get away from the farm, and do what he wanted to do. But right now all he could say to the coach was a lie: "I don't like football."

Dick rarely saw his father; he was a salesman. His father came home every two weeks and spent most of the weekend getting drunk and sobering up. Sometimes he was not ready to go back on the road on time, and this meant that he kept changing jobs. When things were going well, there was plenty of money, and his father was generous with both Dick and his mother. But there were times when there was no money, and it seemed that these times were becoming more frequent.

Dick's mother seemed to be getting more and more jittery, and when she was nervous she jumped on Dick for all sorts of little things. So Dick did not come home directly from school, but put it off as long as possible by staying with his cronies at the drugstore. After supper, he went to his room and pretended to study, or he found an excuse to go out.

Dick had quit going to Sunday school or church when he reached high school, but he still remembered those impossible commandments, including "Honor thy father and thy mother."

Susie was arguing with her mother. As a clincher, she shouted, "But I didn't ask to be born!" Her mother replied, "I know you didn't, my dear. We wanted you very much. That is why your father and I want you to enjoy life to the fullest." Susie suddenly realized that she had a wise and loving mother. We do not choose our parents, but they choose us.

PARENTS IN THE BIBLE

In the Old Testament, the commandment to honor our parents was addressed primarily to adults who have aged parents. It was a warning to an ancient people not to let their aged parents die from exposure or abandonment. This commandment is kept today when we care for our own aged parents.

In the New Testament, this commandment is placed in a new context: "Children, obey your parents in the Lord, for this is right. 'Honor your father and mother' (this is the first commandment with a promise), 'that it may be well with you and that you may live long on the earth.' Fathers, do not provoke your children to anger, but bring them up in the discipline and instruction of the Lord." (Eph. 6:1-4, RSV.)

It is assumed that the parents are Christians, which is why the phrase "in the Lord" is present. Such obedience on the part of children leads to the promise of a long life. But it is not left to the children to decide which parental rules and commands are Christian. It is also assumed that the children are Christians, and Goodspeed's translation says, "As Christians obey your parents" (Eph. 6:1).

The fathers, too, have an obligation not to make their children angry. "You fathers, too," in Goodspeed's translation, "must not irritate your children." "Christian training and instruction" is the goal (Eph. 6:4).

Jewish children rarely end up as juvenile delinquents, and the chief reason is that Jewish family life has specific goals for the parents and the children. A sense of Jewish culture and faith permeates most Jewish families. Parents have a sense of authority. The results show in both freedom from immorality and success in life. Christian families who take their responsibilities seriously also are successful in rearing children who become well-adjusted, loyal Christian adults.

RULES OF THE HOUSE

Modern psychology has helped us to understand this passage from Ephesians. A child needs the security of rules which suit his age. A playpen would be a prison if it had a top on it, but its purpose is not to keep the baby in; it is to keep the world out. Within the playpen, the baby has a world he can handle. As he grows, his world and its rules keep changing. But all along he needs some kind of law and order to have a structure for his life. A small child describes law as "what we do at our house," for the law is a "fence around his freedom." It provides the psychological and social security he needs in order to grow. With increasing maturity, which results from security and freedom, the child begins to develop his own conscience and to accept additional responsibility.

This places on the shoulders of parents the requirement that they bring up their children "in the nurture and admonition of the Lord," or as Proverbs puts it, "Train up a child in the way he should go, and even when he is old, he will not depart from it" (22:6). The moral values, conscience, and Christian insights developed from the beginning are the basis for adult decisions. But one clergyman, preaching on the Proverbs text, modified it as follows: "Train up a child in the way he should go, and when he grows up, he will depart more or less therefrom." This indicates that education in freedom is part of the process, and parents cannot determine how a child will develop.

The parents, with this tremendous responsibility, are far from perfect. They are able to pray, "We have done those things which we ought not to have done, and we have left undone those things which we ought to have done, and there is no health in us." As they kneel in confession, they recognize their own sin and lack of wholeness (health), and their need for foregiveness. But while God may forgive them, he does not take away their responsibility.

Let us now return to John, who cannot play football because he has to work on the farm. He hates the farm and is beginning to hate his father. His father, on the other hand, is limited in what he can do because to run the farm at a profit he needs John's unpaid help. His father also comes from a tradition where the father is the boss and does not need to explain his commands. Because they are caught in a bind, with money the chief problem, there is no way for John to play football. The only hope is that John and his father can come to an understanding of their mutual problem. The father needs to understand John's frustration and smoldering rebellion, even if he cannot relieve the situation; and John needs to understand the spot his father is in. John does not see that his father's problem involves the whole family, including himself.

Dick's problem is much more difficult. He is in a family that lacks the stability of John's family. His father's tensions show up in his drinking and irregular work; his mother's tensions are the result of his father's problems. So Dick finds his solution by escaping from a home situation. Because he cannot enlist his parents in either facing or solving the complex situation, he needs help from either an expert counselor or a pastor.

Susie really does not have a problem. She has met her mother head-on in a conflict, and her mother has been able to resolve the emotional tension as a prelude to facing the problem which needs discussion. The channels of communication have been kept open by the wisdom of the mother, and Susie has responded with shame and understanding.

CAN WE RESPECT OUR PARENTS?

The requirement to honor one's parents is open to several interpretations. John's obedience follows from a situation which cannot be changed. He may be fed up with his father's authoritarian position, but at least he can see that it reflects both his father's previous experience in an authoritarian home and his father's current experience as a farmer. Communication between them is a possibility, but John will have to work at it.

Dick may not respect his father and he may be worried about his mother's nervousness, but neither of them interferes with what he considers his freedom. What he has lost is communication with his parents, both of whom need help before there can be any stability in the family. He has become so irritated, especially with his father, that he has absented himself from home as much as possible. Yet even Dick may honor the roles of fatherhood and motherhood and work for the achievement of both roles for his parents.

Susie loves and understands her mother, and can honor her in the sense of putting her in a place of honor, for her mother has the wisdom to respond with insight and humor to Susie's frustrations.

PARENTS HAVE POWER

Parents are to be honored because they have power. It is almost impossible for the state to take a child away from its mother, no matter how incompetent she is. The decisions that govern the development of the child are made by the parents, and there is no outside check as long as the child is not tortured or maltreated in some extreme way.

Your parents decided whether you would be baptized; you had nothing to say about it. They decided whether the family would move, how large a house you lived in, what kind of clothes you wore, and when you began to go to Sunday school. They made important decisions about your education—public, parochial, or private school; and in some cases they moved to a different school district in order to give you a better opportunity. They decided on your diet, picked out your Christmas and birthday gifts, threw parties, and paid your doctor's bills.

They continue to have this power now. They decide if you need your teeth straightened and pay for it. They have the right to any money you make. They can tell you what work you must do around the house. They grant you an allowance. In most cases, they decide whether you go to work or college when you complete high school.

Legally they are responsible, too. If you are under age and want to be married, your parents must give their signed permission. They must keep you in school until you are sixteen. In some states, they have to co-sign your driver's license.

You are dealing with a power structure that is backed by the law. They are responsible to the law, and so are you. But the law places the power in their hands and not yours. These laws have changed over the years. There was a time in Connecticut when the master of the house had to catechize the servants and children every Sunday, and this was checked by the pastor of the church, who was also an officer of the town meeting. Children have gained more freedom as times have changed, but the source of parental authority is still backed by the law.

When you look back at all the decisions your parents made to help you be what you are today, you must be amazed at their use of this responsibility. Of course they made mistakes, but on the whole they were concerned with your welfare and did the best they could in the circumstances. And they were limited by the fact that they had to work with *you,* with all your quirks, for each person is unique, and they had to make decisions based on both your general welfare and your specific needs.

To honor one's parents means to recognize that they have power to exert authority. They can lock you in your room on weekends, feed you lukewarm soup, and dress you to look like a youngster from the gay nineties. As long as your welfare is not endangered, they can do what they want.

PARENTS AND RELIGION

The Bible is full of advice to children, especially in Proverbs:

> Hear, O sons, a father's instruction,
>   and be attentive, that you may gain insight;
> for I give you good precepts:
>   do not forsake my teaching.
> When I was a son with my father,
>   tender, the only one in the sight of my mother,
> he taught me, and said to me,
> "Let your heart hold fast my words;
>   keep my commandments, and live;
> do not forget, and do not turn away from the words of
>   my mouth.
> Get wisdom; get insight. . . ."
> The fear of the LORD is the beginning of wisdom,
>   and the knowledge of the Holy One is insight.
>
> (Prov. 4:1-5; 9:10, RSV.)

Your early religious upbringing has depended more on your parents than you might expect. Most of your basic attitudes were developed in the early years, when you were under the absolute control of your parents. Your mother not only introduced you to your five senses, but she also created an atmosphere that was free from anxiety, where you had a sense of security. Later on she began to tell you stories, not necessarily religious ones, that helped you answer the questions, "Who am I?" "Who are you?" and "What is the world like?"

Your father probably has not done as much religious teaching as your mother, but he has played an important part. Jesus said: "If you then, who are evil, know how to give good gifts to your children, how much more will your Father who is in heaven give good things to those who ask him?" (Mt. 7: 11.) You learned about the fatherhood of God first from your own father. The important point is that the experience of human fatherhood should help us see the ideal of God as Father.

The parents together do much to create what has been called "an atmosphere in which grace dwells." Some homes are locations for no-decision fights, angry catcalls, and the giant double-cross. But the Christian home seeks to be a cell of the larger body of Christ, even though it is made up of sinners. The kind of love and affection expressed by your father and mother is crucial for an understanding of the text, "We love, because he first loved us" (1 Jn. 4:19).

WE HONOR PARENTHOOD

We honor fatherhood and motherhood before we honor our particular parents. God ordered the world this way, so "let marriage be held in honor among all" (Heb. 13:4). "It is not good that man should be alone. . . . Therefore a man leaves his father and his mother and cleaves to his wife, and they become one flesh." (Gen. 2:18, 24, RSV.)

Parents have a problem that they never clearly understand as they watch their children grow up. How can they withdraw their authority and permit freedom, doing so at the proper rate for the welfare of the particular and unique young people that are involved?

Where, then, do you stand? Parents of young children have unlimited power and authority; but your parents are dealing with a young person who is seeking out a basis for authority in his own life. You are building on the formation of character provided in your home by your parents, and as you seek freedom to move toward maturity you are frustrated by the roadblocks or at least directed by their wishes toward new goals. So obedience and honor are connected, and yet the honor remains when you are grown and they are old. They are *your* parents; they chose you; even though they may be separated by death, divorce, or distance, there is a tie that remains. This we honor throughout life.

rivalry
in
the
family

David was a successful outlaw, a great warrior, a powerful king, and a servant of the Lord. But as a father, his record was full of sordidness, tragedy, and jealousy among his many children. His own record was unsavory by modern standards, for he was underhanded in the way he obtained some of his wives, but he lived in a time when no blame was attached to polygamy or to having concubines. As a result, most of his children were half-brothers and half-sisters.

This large family caused David many heartaches. The story begins with the lovely Tamar, who was raped by her half-brother, Amnon, by a ruse. Absalom, her full-brother, waited three years for a chance to get even, and then had Amnon slain. As a result, Absalom, who was one of David's favorites, fled and stayed in Geshur for three years before his father forgave him and restored him to favor.

Absalom then began a rebellion against David in order to become king; he could not wait for his father's death to inherit the throne. But the king ordered Joab and his other generals, "Deal gently for my sake with the young man Absalom." Absalom's head was caught fast in an oak tree, and he hung there; so Joab put darts into him and his soldiers killed Absalom. When David heard the news, he was overcome with grief, for he loved his rebellious son: "O my son Absalom, my son, my son, Absalom! Would I had died instead of you, O Absalom, my son, my son!" (2 Sam. 18:33, RSV.)

Only fast footwork by Bathsheba established her son, Solomon, as king after Adonijah was expected to succeed David. Solomon moved swiftly to establish the kingdom by purging the opposition, including his half-brother Adonijah and David's effective commander-in-chief, Joab. The new hatchet man was Benaiah.

We do not hear much about other members of the family, for only the outstanding ones are mentioned, and they are outstanding because either they were eliminated or did the eliminating. It is not a pretty picture. David was not a successful father.

DAVID'S FAITH

David, in his way, loved his children. He was willing to forgive them for grievous sins, including rape and murder. Of course, David in the past had been guilty of adultery and of many killings. Yet he, too, was willing to ask God's forgiveness. After he had taken Bathsheba and caused Uriah the Hittite to be killed in action, Nathan had the courage to tell the king the parable of the ewe lamb, and the king was indignant over the incident in the story. At this point, Nathan said, "You are the man!" And David recognized the sin he had committed and said, "I have sinned against the Lord."

The child born to Bathsheba and David became sick. David fasted and prayed; and after a week the baby died. The elders were afraid to tell the king, but he could sense from their manner that the baby was dead.

> Then David arose from the earth, and washed, and anointed himself, and changed his clothes; and he went into the house of the LORD, and worshiped; he then went to his own house; and when he asked, they set food before him, and he ate. Then his servants said to him, "What is this thing that you have done? You fasted and wept for the child while it was alive; but when the

child died, you arose and ate food." He said, "While the
child was still alive, I fasted and wept; for I said, 'Who
knows whether the LORD will be gracious to me, that the
child may live?' But now he is dead; why should I fast?
Can I bring him back again? I shall go to him, but he
will not return to me."

(2 Sam. 12:20-23, RSV.)

Here we see a father in the midst of grief, but he was a man
who lived by faith. He was capable of grievous sins, but also
of repentance and faith. He lived by a code which is shocking
to modern man, but in every crisis he was sustained because
of his faith in God. We are told that the people loved him, and
we can see why. David was a great person as warrior, king,
and father, not because he was a paragon of virtue but because
he was a man of faith.

Not all fathers are like David. Most fathers have higher moral
standards and less authority. A father today is expected to be
the husband of one wife and to have only a few children. He
has much less confusion in his home than did David. But
few fathers exhibit the capacity for repentance and faith which
we see in David at his best.

WHEN CHILDREN FIGHT

What we see in David is his failure to handle the rivalries
among his children. With the mixture of half-brothers and
half-sisters, jealousy was sure to exist and sometimes it could
lead to outright hatred and murder. But this has been known
to happen in a family with one wife and two children, as portrayed in the story of Cain and Abel. We often mess things up,
and everything looks hopeless until God reverses what men
have distorted.

Jim was a high school student who became interested in
model airplanes. The only place where he could have privacy
to work on them was his bedroom. Often he had to leave various pieces of his models around the room, for he worked on
his models at night and had to quit and go to bed while the
process of making a model went on. When he got home from

school, the pieces would be out of order and some of them would be broken. It was clear who the criminal was: his little brother. And he was ready to break his brother's neck.

Jim's mother had not realized how important the parts of the model were, and when she was making Jim's bed in the morning, little Tommy would come into the room with her and play with them. A solution was worked out when Jim talked over his concern with his parents: Jim would make his own bed, keep his own room clean, and have a lock on his door. He knew that Tommy would get in his hair in other ways, but at least Jim would have privacy to work on his models without having everything messed up or broken. The answer to a problem like this is almost always the same: *keep open the channels of communication.*

WHY PRISCILLA CHEATED

Priscilla always got a high grade in her algebra class because she had a system. Her good friend, Ann, was in another section of the class that met earlier in the day, and when there was a test, Ann gave the questions to Priscilla during the lunch hour. The other students knew what was happening but they did not want to tattle. Marian was disturbed about this, especially because the teacher made the work too hard and answered their complaints by saying, "If Priscilla can do it, I don't see why the rest of you have difficulty."

Marian talked to her mother about it, and her mother suggested that she tell Priscilla how the rest of the class felt. That afternoon, there was a gathering of the girls at Priscilla's house, but the music was already going when Marian arrived and nothing was said. After awhile, Priscilla's mother came into the room and looked as if she had something to say. The music was stopped and they looked at her.

"I thought you'd like to hear about Alice," she said. "She has just been elected to Phi Beta Kappa at college." Then she turned to Priscilla. "You'll have to keep getting those good grades in algebra if you are going to keep up with your sister."

After her mother went out of the room, Priscilla's lip trembled and her eyes watered. "I hate her! That sister of mine! It's always Alice the bright one. I've got to be as smart as Alice. I wish she'd break her neck. Then I wouldn't have to cheat to get those good grades!"

The party was ruined and the girls left. When Marian got home, she said to her mother, "No wonder Priscilla has to cheat. Her mother puts unfair pressure on her. But we've got to make her stop. It isn't fair to any of us, including Priscilla."

Cheating is often the result of pressure. In Priscilla's case, the pressure came from her mother. Alice was successful in school and therefore was held up as a model to Priscilla. Priscilla was a good student, but could not possibly match her sister. Yet she believed that the only way she could gain her mother's and father's approval was to get good grades by fair means or foul.

Priscilla recognized that Alice was the apple of her parents' eyes. Parents sometimes play favorites. They may think that they show their love equally, but they take pride in their children's achievements, and therefore they tend to hold up their most successful child as an example for the rest of the family. Usually this unfair competition is an unintentional thing, but that does not make it any easier on the children who suffer from it. It leads to frustration and sometimes to cheating as an easy way out.

ALL CHILDREN ARE DIFFERENT

Even when parents are wise enough to avoid making comparisons, the children can see the difference in their own achievements. They compare their report cards. They make snide remarks about each other. Attempts by the parents to provide a balanced view are rejected by the children, for they know they live in a competitive world and have to make good. The competition to get into college, or just to graduate from high school, can lead to the temptation to cheat, to the dislike of successful rivals, and to the hatred of brothers and sisters.

After Solomon had successfully manipulated his way to his father's throne, with a big assist from his mother Bathsheba, he knew that in order to stay on top he had to get rid of his rivals, chiefly his half-brother Adonijah who thought he was the rightful successor. Adonijah had been next in line after Absalom and had strong backing. As long as Adonijah lived, he would be a rival, so he was eliminated. This is the way Priscilla felt about Alice.

The same kind of rivalry is illustrated in the story of Cain and Abel. Abel, the younger brother, was a sheepherder, and Cain was a farmer. The Lord preferred the offering of sheep to the offering of fruit. But the Lord made it clear that he had not rejected Cain, for, "If you do well, will you not be accepted?" But Cain enticed his brother into the field and killed him. Cain asked, "Am I my brother's keeper?" So Cain was banished from the presence of the Lord, although he was marked so that no man would kill him, and he brought up his family in a foreign land.

So Cain and Abel, Absalom and Amnon, Solomon and Adonijah, Priscilla and Alice, you and your brother or sister, have these same thoughts from time to time. The tendency is to place the blame for such thoughts on your parents. After all, they gave you your inheritance; after all, they favor one child or another. So it is not your fault if you have feelings of hostility toward your brother or sister or parents. But this excuse does not solve your problem.

YOUR SENSE OF SELF-ACCEPTANCE

One of the most important things a young person needs is a sense of self-acceptance. When we are treated unfairly or are misunderstood, this is a difficult achievement, but it is hard enough even when everything is going right.

Priscilla was trying to be somebody she was not. She was not Alice. And even though her mother wanted her to be like Alice, Priscilla needed to know who she was. She was a person who had certain abilities, interests, and potentialities. These were peculiarly hers, and they were different from Alice's. But as long as she bowed to the pressure to be like Alice, she would continue to cheat and try to be somebody she was not. So her outward "personage" and her inner "person" were at odds. She appeared to her friends with a mask that disguised who she really was, and this mask fooled even herself, for she did not know herself.

Her mother was no help. Her mother was trying to force her into an image that did not fit. So Priscilla needed help that she could not get from her parents or her friends. What would help her was the lesson that God loves us as we are. Even Cain was told that if he did well, God would accept him, and this means that Cain was expected to be himself and to do well as a farmer, in terms of his own potentialities. Once you accept the fact that God accepts you as you are, you are on the road to maturity.

If Priscilla had learned this one Christian truth, she would have been helped to be her true self, even with all the pressure from her mother to be like Alice. This would have helped her overcome her hatred of Alice, her temptation to cheat, and her slavery to being like someone other than herself. No longer would Alice be a rival, for Priscilla would be free to be her own self. If she had one talent and Alice had five, this would make no difference.

HOW MANY TALENTS HAVE YOU?

Jesus told a story of three men. A man entrusted his property to them: "To one he gave five talents, to another two, to another one, to each according to his ability. Then he went away." (Mt. 25:15, RSV.) A talent, which was a measure of weight, was worth about $1,000 in silver or gold. The men with $5,000 and $2,000 invested their money and made more, but the man with $1,000 buried his for safekeeping. When the master returned, he praised those who invested their money, but he cast out the one who buried his. The third man was afraid.

From this story, the word "talent" has come into our language in terms of aptitudes. You are not condemned because you are not richly talented and you are not praised for having great talents. If you fail to use the gifts God has given you, whether it be one talent or five, then you are condemned. Self-acceptance is based on self-knowledge and on faith in God.

SOME IDEAS THAT MAY HELP YOU

Try going through the following statements of who God is and what he does for you. You may find it frustrating; you may find such propositions too great for your belief. But in the midst of rivalry with brothers and sisters, of difficulties with parents, and of problems in your own development, you will move toward self-knowledge and self-acceptance if you take these beliefs and attitudes seriously.

Self-knowledge grows as knowledge of God grows. This was David's strength in spite of all his failures and sins. When I discover that I am a creature and that *God is my Creator,* I know that God made me the way I am and that he is at work in me. This helps me to overcome my anxieties and use my talents as fully as possible. I do this, but at the same time God does it through me.

When I say that *God is the Father almighty,* this means that God has all the power there is. In him I find the answer to my search for courage that conquers my uncertainty. My anxiety does not disappear, but I am able to accept myself as I am.

When I pray to *God who is eternal,* I am saying that for God everything is present, for he is beyond time. I am worried about the past I can remember, about the present that I experience, and about the future that I anticipate. Because God is eternal, all the moments of time are united in eternity. Therefore, I hope for eternal life.

When I find that *God is present everywhere,* I have the courage to live with myself and with others and to accept the realities of life. I can pray:

> "O God, give me the serenity to accept what cannot be changed; give me the courage to change what can be changed; and the wisdom to distinguish the one from the other. Amen."

[1] Reinhold Niebuhr.

When I agree that *God is all-knowing,* the dark and hidden things in my life are brought to light. I know that nothing can be concealed from God. This may make me uncomfortable, but because I have faith in him this gives me hope as well.

Finally, when I become mature enough to know that *God is love,* I come into a personal relationship with him. God's self-giving love is a mystery to me, although I see it in the life and death and resurrection of Jesus Christ. I know that God seeks me, but that I must take the first step.

> I sought the Lord, and afterward I knew
> He moved my soul to seek him, seeking me;
> It was not I that found, O Saviour true;
> No, I was found of thee.[2]

[2] Anonymous, "I sought the Lord."

the right to rebel

Peter went out of the house, slamming the door. He jumped into the car, started it and put it in gear and pulled away from the curb with screeching tires. He was angry. He had asked his father for an advance on his allowance, which he needed badly, and the old man had turned him down flat.

Pete's allowance was not very big, and his jalopy ate up a lot of gasoline. He had promised to pick up some of the fellows that evening, and he did not want to sponge off them for gas. But his father had said, "Nothing doing." It was hard enough to get his regular allowance out of his father, but an advance was an impossibility. He did not understand how his father could be so stingy about money. His friends had bigger allowances and could get advances in emergencies, but he was stuck.

Pete had worked the past summer to earn enough money for the car and the insurance. He thought this extra insurance premium for those under twenty-five was unfair, but his father had insisted that Pete earn enough to cover it before he could buy a car. So Pete had no savings, just his allowance, and the car ate up everything he got. But his father showed no sympathy. He just said, "It's your car and you're stuck with it."

Pete burned the tires rounding a corner and pulled up at the drugstore. He usually did not let his feelings about his Dad show when he was with his friends, but this time he could not keep quiet.

What Pete did not know was that his father was having business troubles. There just was not enough money to go round, so Pete's allowance was small and there were no extras. But his father was proud and would not admit that he could not afford to give Pete a bigger allowance. Secretly, he was proud of Pete for making enough money during the summer to buy an old car and to cover the insurance, but he would not admit it. Pete's mother had to struggle on a small household budget and managed to make ends meet by clever marketing. Both of his parents believed that Pete would learn the value of money if he had no opportunity to be extravagant, for they assumed that Pete would probably stay in the same income group when he was on his own.

But none of this had been communicated to Pete, so he was hot and bothered about his stingy parents. But before he could blurt out his feelings to his friends, they asked him:

"Have you heard about Buck?"

Buck was the son of the wealthiest family that Pete knew, went to the same church, dressed well, and drove a Corvette. Buck always had enough spending money, and often he would blow some of it to treat the whole gang. He was well liked.

"He's in trouble. Seems he drove over the border with Janie last night and they got some hooch, and on the way home he was driving too fast and a copper chased him. Buck opened up the Corvette and left the cop behind, but he took a turn too fast and rolled his car. Neither of them was hurt, but the cop got him for everything in the book. Now his old man is trying to get the charges quashed."

"It's easy come and easy go."

"Yeah. Buck's got everything a fellow wants. Money grows like weeds in his family. He never had to work for any of it. But what good would it have been if he or Janie had been hurt or killed?"

Pete listened to this conversation among his friends and decided that he would not say anything about his parents.

DO YOU WANT REBELLION OR INDEPENDENCE?

Adolescence is sometimes called the period of the "war of independence." But often it is more a "war of rebellion." Our Revolutionary War was called both: to the colonists it was a fight for independence; to the English it was simply rebellion. Independence means learning to stand on your own feet, to use your freedom with responsibility, to make decisions that take into account the wishes of your parents and others.

Rebellion, on the other hand, is doing the opposite of what those in authority want. You rebel against your parents by figuring out their desires and then deliberately doing the opposite. But if you rebel in this way, your conduct is determined as much by your parents as if you were obedient. Shrewd parents have been known to use with younger children the technique of expressing desires opposite to their real wishes, in order to achieve what they want; and this is not unknown among the desperate parents of some mule-like young people. There is no freedom when what you do is determined by the reverse of what your parents want.

This struggle for determination, for independence, which reaches such a peak during adolescence, can continue without conflict with your parents, and it continues after you have left home either for a job or college. To some extent, all of your decisions will be determined by your wish to please others, and this goes on all through life, unless you want to be a hermit.

But the question arises: Whom shall you please? Your close friend? The gang? Your parents? Your future mate? Your boss? God? Yourself?

AN APPROACH TO DATING

Take the problems that arise from boy-girl relations. Marcia's mother had warned her about boys. Boys were always ready to "make out." Good girls did not give the boys any satisfaction at all. But when Marcia was out with an interesting boy, she discovered that she wanted him to kiss her. She liked the thrills of necking. But because of her mother's attitude, she always felt a sense of guilt, even though she did not believe what she was doing was wrong, for she always stopped before the going got rough. Marcia had developed her own point of view. She always tried to treat the boys she knew as persons. She did not use them to satisfy her own vanity or to show them off to the other girls or to make another boy jealous. When she kissed a boy, she did it because she liked him and believed that he liked her. And when a boy tried to use her for his own pleasure, she stopped him cold. She said, "I wouldn't respect you or myself if I let you do this."

But she still felt guilty about it, because she knew her mother would disapprove of her actions. She was working out a philosophy on the basis of respect for others, and she was strong enough not to try to buy popularity through necking or to go along with the gang because "everyone does it."

During her senior year in high school, Marcia fell in love with Jack. They talked about the time when they would be married, but Marcia knew that they would have to wait awhile. They became "engaged to be engaged" and did not date anyone else. They talked about their future life together. But first Jack needed some additional training and a job that would support them.

As time went on and they spent more evenings together, their emotions were harder to control. They talked seriously about premarital intercourse, considered the arguments for it and against it. Both of them felt powerful urges. Marcia did not want to talk with her mother about this problem, because her mother had not been particularly helpful when she was working out a philosophy of boy-girl relations in high school. And Marcia knew that while Jack would never take advantage of her, he would do what she decided. So they talked about her philosophy.

"What I decided when I started dating," said Marcia, "was that I would try to act as a person who treated others as persons. I wasn't going to use them for my pleasure, and I wasn't going to be used by them. Whatever we did, I wanted to have them as friends I could respect. I've always believed that people should wait until they are married to have intercourse, but I didn't know why. I know many people don't wait."

She stopped for a minute to gather her thoughts. "Remember, Jack," she continued, "when we heard about that man, Martin Buber, who wrote about the 'I-Thou' relationship? He said that no man should ever use another as a thing, as a means, but always treat him as a person who has his own dignity and rights. If we give in now, I'd be using you for my own pleasure, and you'd be using me."

Jack thought about this. "Is that why men want to marry virgins?" he asked.

"That's why my mother tried so hard to protect me, I think," said Marcia. "She just made the problem extreme, so that I didn't listen to her. But it made me think things through this way."

The conversation veered away from this topic and then Jack asked about Peg and Jim, who were to be married the next week.

"They had to get married," he said.

"I know," replied Marcia. "I talked to Peg about it. She said her mother harped on sex all the time and warned her about boys. But Peg thinks her mother hates her, and she never sees her father. She just doesn't feel loved by anyone. She told me she started playing around with sex just to get even with her mother, and anyhow it made her feel that she was loved by the fellows. Jim just got caught as the father, that's all; and he probably can't be sure."

"Peg must think she's gotten even with her mother," said Jack.

"Peg's ashamed of herself now, because everyone knows why they're getting married in the middle of the term. Her mother hardly speaks to her. Jim isn't happy about it, because it means he can't go on to college next year."

"But lots of the fellows and girls try it and never get pregnant," said Jack.

"That's not the problem," replied Marcia. "Lots of us know how not to get pregnant. But we still have to live with ourselves, and later on with our husbands or wives. God made sex as something attractive and holy, but he provided rules so that people won't hurt each other through a sense of guilt."

Marcia leaned over and kissed Jack. "I think we are on the right track, darling. I'm going to try to talk it over with Mom. Maybe she knows more about this than I thought she did."

ARE COMMANDMENTS SILLY?

Parents have years of experience behind them. This may make them seem stuffy or rigid or opinionated, but sometimes they are standing for the moral law which has its roots in God himself.

"Why should I obey any silly commandments?" Bob asked his father. "Why should I be moral? Thou shalt not steal or kill or lie or cheat or commit—er, commit adultery. These are just man-made laws, and you find it convenient to use them to back up your parental authority."

"That's not the way it is," said Dad. "These commandments come down from the Old Testament. Every code of law is based on them. The courts can put people in jail for breaking them."

Bob had been reading about some of these things and had his arguments ready. "But let's look at history. It was all right for David's soldiers to steal everything they could lay their hands on, to kill everybody left in a village, and to rape the women. Soldiers from Christian countries do the same thing. Soldiers are taught to lie when they are made prisoners. And cheating—hah! It's considered a game in Italy to cheat on your income tax. Even you use every loophole you can think of every April."

"But just because David's soldiers or our soldiers are forced into a war and then are less than human, doesn't make it right, Bob."

"The dean of a law school was arrested for cheating on his income tax. David and Bathsheba had nothing on some people who have lots of wives—only one after the other. And people stand around to see celebrities who steal other people's mates. Dad, it's all a lot of hokum. I've read about those Kinsey reports, and nobody takes sex ethics seriously any more. You know what they say in the business world, 'Do the others before they do you,' and 'Honesty is the best policy as long as it works,' and 'Follow Christ and go broke.' It's like that TV show, everyone is looking out for 'The Imperial Me'!"

"But, Bob, what you are doing is outlining what's wrong with people. Just because many people do something, that doesn't make it right. For example, if murder increased until the police couldn't solve the crime, would you want murderers to go free?"

"No, but—"

"If a man raped your little sister, just because he had a strong urge, would you—?"

"But, Dad, that's different."

"No it isn't, Bob. Would you want your mother to have an affair with some handsome guy while I'm on a trip?"

"No, but—"

"If you were running a store, would you like it if every customer was looking for a way to steal something, or cheat you with a counterfeit bill; or if your cashier was pocketing some of the cash?"

"No, but—"

"No buts about it. This world runs smoothly because most people have moral standards. Wall Street would crash in a day if a broker's word wasn't as good as a written contract. The government couldn't collect income tax if the majority weren't honest. I couldn't let your sister go out on dates if I thought every boy was going to take advantage of her. I wouldn't let you have the car if I thought you were going to get drunk, or drive carelessly, and perhaps kill somebody. If your mother couldn't trust me when I'm travelling, how long do you think our marriage would last? And what happens to cheaters at school when they are caught? And even if they are not caught in high school, how well do they do at work or in college when they don't have the knowledge that their grades show? I tell you, Son, this morality business is simply the ball bearings that keep society running smoothly. And because some people are not moral, we have cops, and judges, and jails."

"Maybe people are mostly naturally good."

"Yeah. Have you read *Lord of the Flies?* How do these nice simple British schoolboys end up? Naturally good, you say? And if you use your moral judgment when you read some of those Bible stories you mentioned, such as David and his soldiers, or Joseph and his brothers, or Lot and his daughters, who was naturally good?"

"All right, some people end up good and some people end up bad. But the good people put the bad people in jail, and in different countries they have different ideas of good and bad. It's all right for Moslems to have several wives at once."

"It was all right for Solomon, too, Bob. But we know what the Christian law is. And as Christians we believe this is superior to other laws."

"Christians are superior?"

"We believe that in the New Testament there are principles of behavior that place a claim on all men. They come down to two points—"

"Love God and love your neighbors," broke in Bob. "I've heard that one. But that's asking too much. Even you don't do that, Pop. How about those kids down the street you wouldn't let us play with? How about your battle against integrating the school in our neighborhood? It was all right in other parts of town, but not in our district. And how about—"

"O.K., Son, I'm not perfect. I've made plenty of mistakes as a parent and citizen and businessman. But at least, I have something to measure my failures against."

"What?"

"Two things: the moral law that we've been talking about, and which you've convicted me of breaking. I plead guilty. But there is one other thing. As a Christian, I believe that God has forgiven me and will forgive me. Because I trust in God, my relationship with him is not broken."

"Is this why you go to church?"

"I think so. That's where I hear the good news and where I can confess my sins and hear the assurance that God forgives me. If Christ died and rose again for me, when I become dead in spirit I am made alive again. That's what Christianity is all about. It's the source of strength for living with the same attitude Christ had. We don't succeed but we keep trying. But we know God has forgiven us through Jesus Christ."

"I've heard this all my life, Dad, but now it begins to make a little more sense."

"It's what we've tried to teach you, Bob, but it comes slowly to all of us. I was in college before I began to see clearly what it means. I don't think anyone ever catches the real meaning of faith until he's about your age, maybe older."

"How do we learn it?"

"I think it comes first in the relationships a child has with his parents. They minister to him as a child, and all he can do is have faith in his parents. He trusts them as they impart their love to him. But sometimes he feels separated from them, dead to them as the New Testament would say, and then he comes alive again through their love. Later on, it can be told in words, but at first it is through relationships. But he probably doesn't really see it until he realizes that God has been working through this love and forgiveness and restoration of relationship. Then he feels 'like a new man' and gains a sense of direction, a desire to be worthy of his calling."

"It's still not clear, but this helps. Maybe there is something to this morality and religion stuff. It seems to make sense to you anyhow."

permissive parents

Mr. and Mrs. Jones were talking about their son, Mike. They were intelligent parents who had read books on "How to Get Along with Your Teenager," and they wanted to give Mike as much freedom as possible.

"You know how repression can ruin a boy," said Mrs. Jones. "We mustn't do anything that will hurt his self-confidence. If we just leave him alone, he can work things out. If we keep telling him what not to do, it will build up a superego that will restrict his activities."

"I don't know what a superego is," said Mr. Jones, "but I wish he would be of some help around the house. You let him get away with anything."

"But if I crack down on him, he will think I don't love him."

"Nonsense. He needs some supervision, some rules, and some hard work. We let him go out on school nights when there is homework to do. We don't even ask him to shovel snow or cut the lawn. When he has a date, we don't know who the girl is."

"But if we're going to be permissive, we have to let him do what he wants."

"He takes the car and goes off God knows where. We don't know. I find empty beer cans on the floor of the car. He runs through his allowance like it's water and you always can find an extra five spot for him."

"He seems to be enjoying himself."

"Anybody enjoys a bit of hell-raising. But it's not good for him. By being *this* permissive, I think we're saying to him that we don't care what he does. We're ducking our responsibility as parents by throwing too much responsibility on him.

That's not real permissiveness, and it isn't parental love. It just saves us the agony of arguments, of using our authority, and he is drifting because we haven't given him any guide lines."

A discussion like this might go on among many parents who are unsure about their roles. Both Mr. and Mrs. Jones were concerned about Mike, but they were puzzled about the guidance they should give, the rules they should enforce, and the pressure they should put on him. Mike, on the other hand, had so much freedom that he was beginning to drift. He had no real purpose, except to enjoy himself. His grades began to suffer. He loafed and had fun, but he was not finding any discipline from his parents and therefore was not developing the self-discipline he needed in order to be a responsible person. He was beginning to think that his parents didn't care what he did, and therefore that they didn't love him. He was losing his sense of security, his sense of belonging, and his feeling for the parent-son relationship. He wasn't really free, because he had lost the foundation of freedom which lies in sound relationships with people.

SOME PARENTS ARE INDIFFERENT

Nancy's parents were not bothered by Mr. Jones's questions. They took Mrs. Jones's position and carried it even further. Mr. Smith commuted from the suburbs and did not get home until late, and therefore Mrs. Smith had all of the responsibility for Nancy and her brothers and sisters. Mrs. Smith was involved in community and church activities and did not have much time to think about Nancy. As a result, Nancy suffered from both indifference and overindulgence. Her mother did not care what Nancy did, as long as it did not cause trouble, and Nancy was allowed to have the car and money for clothes and recreation. There was no check on who her friends were.

Occasionally, Mrs. Smith would let Nancy have a party at home, but on a weekend evening, when Mr. and Mrs. Smith would be at a party elsewhere. Nancy's friends had the run of the house. The parties were usually boisterous but innocent, even though the liquor closet was open. Occasionally one or more of the boys got drunk, but they managed to get home safely.

Then came the night when there was an accident on the way home. The car went off the road, and one of the girls was killed. The boy was arrested for drunken driving and negligent homicide. Investigation led to the information that liquor had been available to minors at the party, and Mr. and Mrs. Smith were arrested for serving liquor to minors. Their defense was that they had not been present at the party, but they admitted that the party had been at their house with their consent, and that the liquor was available. They claimed that they were not responsible, however, because the young people were old enough to make their own decisions, and all or most of them had liquor available in their own homes.

You can duplicate this story, with variations, from almost any newspaper. Sometimes the result is not the death of a girl but the wrecking of the house or the sex play that leads to tragedy. It is news like this that gives a black name to all teenagers, although only a small percentage are involved in this kind of activity.

YOU ARE RESPONSIBLE

There are two points to be drawn from such stories. The first is that young people are responsible for their actions, even when there is lack of supervision. The driver of the death car was convicted, or the vandals were punished, or the sexual damage was permanent. The young people had to live with their misdeeds and take the consequences. Whether they found any solace in their Christian faith we do not know, but we do know that there is forgiveness and the opportunity for a new start, although this does not eliminate the consequences of an act.

The second point is that the parents were also at fault, which is why they were tried and found guilty. The parents, in their lack of concern, indifference, and refusal to provide supervision, had abdicated, even though they excused themselves in the name of permissiveness. There had been a breakdown in communication between the young people and their parents.

CONFIDING IN PARENTS IS DIFFICULT

Many young people have difficulty in confiding in their parents. Back in 1826, John Stuart Mill was feeling depressed, and he wrote, "My father, to whom it would have been natural to me to have recourse in any practical difficulties, was the last person to whom, in such a case as this, I looked for help. Everything convinced me that he had no knowledge of any such mental state as I was suffering from, and that even if he could understand it, he was not the physician who could heal it."

This is the way Nancy felt about her parents, who were so deeply involved in their own activities that they had no time for her. They were so far out of touch with her world that their occasional conversations were civil and on the surface, but there was no opportunity to dig into the deep issues of Nancy's life. Nancy had long ago given up the effort to have confidential conversations with her parents, and now that they were in trouble along with her there was no basis for communication. But the shock of the aftermath of the party might have been sufficient to draw them together and to restore a relationship long since lost.

HOW PERMISSIVE DO YOU WANT YOUR PARENTS TO BE?

When you want your parents to be permissive, what do you mean by this? Is Mrs. Jones's fear of providing obstructions to Mike's wishes a form of permissiveness, or is she just afraid of unpleasantness? Is the Smiths' ignorance of Nancy's activities a form of permissiveness, or is it just indifference?

There is a relationship between permissiveness, freedom, the law, and responsibilty. It is much more complex than most parents or young people think.

When a father lets his son or daughter drive the car on a highway when he or she is below the legal age, the father and the driver are going against the law. After the young person has qualified for a license and has shown himself responsible, it is proper in many cases for the young person to use the car with permission, to have his own keys, and in some cases to carry a gasoline credit card. When a father gives his son or daughter the keys, he is saying, "I trust you."

When a parent serves liquor to his own young people, he is the proper judge as to the age at which this is to be done, but he has no right to serve other young people until they have reached the legal age. He also has the right to refuse to have liquor in his home.

YOUR FREEDOM AND RESPONSIBILITY

Mary and Jane, two friends, were discussing the problems they had in their relationships with their parents.

"My parents are permissive," said Mary. "They try to give me the amount of freedom I can handle with responsibilty. They trust me. But if I can't handle that much responsibility, they will move in with some controls. They will let me use the car when it's free, but not to pick up boys. They will let me date the boys I want, but they insist on meeting them when the boys come for me. They let me set my own study hours, but there are no dates on school nights. When we were younger, there was no TV on school nights, so we never got into the habit, but as a senior I can watch TV if I think it won't interfere with my homework. I tried baby-sitting while doing my homework, but we gave that up when it didn't work out right; some girls can do it, but I can't, so no more baby-sitting on school nights. So we have a combination of flexible rules and lots of freedom, and we can negotiate when things get rough."

"How do you handle hours for coming in after dates?" asked Jane.

"We agree on the late hours, with the understanding that a few minutes one way or the other doesn't matter. What they don't want is fast driving to make a deadline. We have an agreement that if there is trouble, or if the boy that is driving is drinking, I can phone them and they will come for me. The only time this happened, another boy who was sober drove me home."

"My parents are a lot like yours," replied Jane, "except that they always give me pep talks. Mother, especially, has set speeches before every date, warning me about the possible dangers. The trouble is, none of the dangers ever occur. The boys don't drink, they don't try to go too far, and they get me home on time. I wish Mother knew how nice most of the boys are. I don't want to go out with the wild ones anyhow, but she thinks I do."

In this conversation we see exhibited specific instances of Christian parents who trust their young people. Freedom is real, because it operates within limits clearly defined by flexible rules. As the young people get older, the rules are changed to match the situations.

Betty had a midnight curfew most of her senior year, but it had been changed to two o'clock for the spring dance. Now came the high school senior prom, which in this town had the tradition of dancing until four and then breakfast. Betty's parents were not sure they liked the idea, but they consulted with other parents and arrangements were made for the parents to serve the breakfast. There were parents at the ball, and others at the breakfast to see that all went well. Everyone was in bed by six in the morning, and some fathers were groggy at work on Saturday.

HOW MUCH OOMPH HAVE YOU?

When you were little, your parents took some long chances. When you were learning to walk, you had some falls. The first time you went up the steps to go down the slide, you might have fallen. The first time you climbed a tree, you could have broken your neck. And you could have slipped off the roof. Long before adolescence, children explore and take risks. Some parents overprotect their children, so that the risks are less but the rewards are nil; some parents provide no guidance, so that adventure is great but accidents are frequent and sometimes fatal; and some parents try to keep the proper balance, so that there is plenty of adventure and calculated risk.

Some young people get along well with their parents because they don't have enough oomph to rebel. We see this in so-called well-adjusted young people, who get good grades, go to church, and stay out of trouble. A study of their goals showed that they are not interested in travel, adventurous jobs, or any kind of risk. They are content to be stick-in-the-muds. The high level of parental understanding, readiness to accept the church's teachings, and good citizenship in school seems to mark them for overpassivity. They come to like security, and lose their concern for others.

This is a strange paradox. You want to get along with your parents, avoid necessary conflict, do well in school, and have friends, but this may be so secure a way of living that you no longer want to explore the world, take risks, and find excitement in unusual kinds of achievement. You should know that young people who are much troubled by their parents are more likely to explore new worlds, although they may be doing so to escape an unpleasant situation.

Parents who are permissive in the right sense may help you at this point. They can assist you in thinking through goals that are not routine, they can stimulate your imagination in terms of travel, of jobs that take you to foreign places, of joining the Peace Corps, even of finding summer jobs at distant resorts.

HOW TO BE ADVENTURESOME

The church can help you to be adventuresome. You have probably mapped out the travels of St. Paul sometime during your Sunday school experience. He was willing to leave his Jewish faith, support himself as a tentmaker, and to travel to the ends of the known world to bring the gospel to the heathen. He enlisted the companionship of Barnabas, Timothy, Mark, and others on these adventures, and they experienced imprisonment, beatings, shipwreck, and every kind of discomfort as they carried on their task.

The Letter to the Hebrews lists those who were known for

their faith. They include remarkable people from the Old Testament, none of whom had an easy life. Then as we come through history, there were Christians who were burned, who were thrown to the lions, who took dangerous chances and came out whole. Martin Luther took on most of Christendom, including the Pope, and ended up with a wife and six children, and in the process he turned the Christian world inside out. Mild-mannered Thomas Cranmer, who was a statesman and archbishop, finally was burned at the stake. There were missionaries in recent years who took great risks in going to foreign countries, and some have recently lost their lives in the Congo. St. Paul wrote his best letters while residing in jail, and so did Martin Luther King, Jr.

Young people today are not content to stand aside in comfort while others take chances. The Peace Corps, Operation Cross Roads Africa, the many organizations of students working on the racial problem, the students who risked and even lost their lives in Mississippi, are examples of what you are capable of.

REBELS WITHOUT A CAUSE?

There is another kind of risk. The rebels who are fighting against society, who are called "rebels without a cause," who have nothing to fight for so they fight against everything, come from all levels of society. Mostly they have experienced broken homes, alcoholism among their parents, inconsistent discipline and authority, sometimes living in overcrowded flats and sometimes in magnificent mansions. What they have lacked is a consistent parental love. So they seek gratification in any form of pleasure they can find.

But even this is a dangerous generalization, for there are children who grow up in homes where parents do not love them and who still make good. Somewhere along the way, a glimmer of light breaks through and they begin to see clearly what their goals are. Often it is a teacher at school or Sunday school, a youth group leader, or a friend of the family who shows them the way. So we are never without hope.

Most parents are concerned about their children, even when they seem distracted by other interests. With this concern, they are sometimes confused, for in this complex world decisions are not easily reached. Furthermore, they do not change as fast as your needs do. But if you know this, you can help your parents to understand you, and then they will be able to assist you at your point of need. This is the crucial point, and you are the one who can do something about it.

your family and your future work

If we look at Jesus and his family as portrayed in the Gospels and without any presuppositions about the mystery of his birth, we find a picture that is helpful for young people today.

The story starts with the trip to Jerusalem when Jesus had entered adolescence. You can imagine how exciting it was to go from the village of Nazareth to the big city. He may have been there before, but at this age there would be new sights and people and concerns. He was old enough to be independent of his parents and go where he wanted. His parents supposed that he would join the caravan when it was time to leave for Nazareth and did not bother to check until the end of the first day.

But Jesus was so interested in questioning the rabbis that he paid no attention to time. When Joseph and Mary could not find him in the caravan, they returned to Jerusalem and finally located him in one of the outer courts of the temple, where a conversation was going on. His parents were astonished at what had happened and his mother asked, "My son, why have you treated us like this? Your father and I have been searching for you in great anxiety." (Lk. 2:48, NEB.) His answer confused them, for he asked, "Did you not know that I was bound to be in my Father's house?" So he returned with them to Nazareth, where he "continued to be under their authority."

As far as relations with his parents went, this was not much

64

different from a boy who gets so excited at a mechanical exhibit at the World's Fair that he misses the bus for home. Jesus, like any other boy, "grew big and strong and full of wisdom," and as he came to know himself and his interests he naturally sought out the wise men in his field and asked questions. His questions were so penetrating that they were amazed.

This beginning of independence comes in adolescence. In order for Jesus to be on his own in Jerusalem, his parents had had to give him a great deal of freedom, as was proper. But they expected him to rejoin them at the appointed time. This is the way every growing person achieves freedom: his parents seek to provide freedom of opportunity and decision, but they expect him to meet his responsibilities. The more responsible he becomes, the more freedom he can be given. But in Jesus' case, there was already evident a higher calling, an obedience to his Father which was more than obedience to Joseph and Mary. This, his parents could not understand. Quite properly, as an adolescent, he returned home with them and "continued to be under their authority."

FAMILY OPPOSITION TO A CAREER

The next picture the Gospels provide is after Jesus established a reputation as a teacher and healer, when he was about thirty. He was accused of casting out demons through the power of the prince of demons, and finally people began to say he was "out of his mind" (Mk. 3:21, NEB), "deranged" or "mad." So his family came to take charge of him, for they seemed to believe it, too. When they arrived, there was such a crowd that they had to send him a message, "Your mother and your brothers are outside asking for you." His reply was a rebuke to them: "Who is my mother? Who are my brothers?" Then he made a point which moved his listeners beyond the family circle: "Here are my mother and my brothers. Whoever does the will of God is my brother, my sister, my mother." (Mk. 3:33–35, NEB.)

The story stops there. We can assume that he did not go home with them. He defended himself against his accusers ("How can Satan cast out Satan?") and proceeded with his ministry of teaching and healing.

Later on he returned home to Nazareth, and again he ran into trouble. There was a large congregation in the synagogue and they were amazed and asked, "Where does he get it from?" They could not understand how he had attained such wisdom and the power to perform miracles, for they knew who he was: "Is he not the carpenter's son? Is not his mother called Mary, his brothers James, Joseph, Simon and Judas? And are not his sisters here with us? Where then has he got all this from?" When they "fell foul of him," he was led to say, "A prophet will always be held in honour, except in his town, and in his own family." So he left his home town, where their lack of faith made his ministry impossible. (Mt. 13:53–58, NEB.)

We can speculate on why Jesus was not popular in Nazareth or in his own family. One possibility is that no one could conceive of any inhabitant of Nazareth, with all of its limitations, rising to the status of a prophet and healer, especially when his family members were known to them. In his family there may have been resentment because Jesus had not continued to work at his trade and support the others. But we do not know. The record is clear on only one point, and that is the opposition to Jesus' ministry in his own home. None of his family appeared in the story again until after the crucifixion, when they became followers of "The Way," and his brother James became the leader of the church in Jerusalem.[1]

A FATHER'S ROLE

In this record, there was a forgotten man. Joseph was mentioned in the birth stories and in the account of the boy Jesus

---

[1] See *I Remember Jesus*, by Randolph C. Miller, New York: Seabury Press, 1958, for a fuller interpretation. The only reference to Jesus' mother at the crucifixion is John 19:25.

in the temple. Jesus was called "the carpenter's son" in Matthew. Then Joseph vanished. He was cited in order to show that Jesus' ancestry went back to David. Joseph took care of a family of at least five boys and two girls; he was a simple workman and a descendant of David. Out of his family came Jesus, who is the Savior of the world, James, who was the leader of the Jewish-Christian community in Jerusalem, and his young wife, Mary, who is venerated by all Christians.

It is likely that Mary was very young, in her teens, when Jesus was born. Joseph was probably much older. When Joseph died, Jesus may have taken over the work of a carpenter and supported the large family. So when Jesus quit his work to become a teacher and healer after his baptism, at about the age of thirty, the family was opposed to this because it meant the loss of income.

Joseph must have been a remarkable person. If Jesus as a boy learned about human fatherhood, it must have been from Joseph. Jesus used illustrations of human fatherhood in his teaching to explain what the divine Father is like. When Jesus spoke of fatherhood, this concept had more of tenderness and love in it than we find in the Oriental patriarch. This analogy of God as Father tells us much about God, but perhaps it tells us something also about Joseph. As Jesus spoke of God as Father, we know that behind the scene was Joseph. In the story of the Prodigal Son, the loving and forgiving father welcomes the lost son and sets up a banquet for him. Is this what Joseph would have done if one of his sons had wandered from the fold? But after Joseph was dead, the rest of the family could not understand that Jesus had a job to do.

DOCTOR OR MINISTER?

It is helpful for you to know that Jesus had problems with his parents. The process of growing up leads to tensions, to differences of opinion, and sometimes to arguments about what lies in the future.

Bill was the son of a doctor. The family was active in the church. Bill's father had always wanted Bill to be a doctor, and this was taken for granted by all the family. Even Bill had never seriously considered anything else as a vocation. But then Bill went to a summer church conference; he met some ministers who were normal persons, masculine, athletic, and dedicated; and as the summer wore on, Bill began to have thoughts about the ordained ministry. Bill knew that as a doctor he could be a Christian, but he was less sure that he had the skills and the interests to be a surgeon, which was what his father wanted. He liked working with people, he was capable of leadership, and he was a good speaker. Perhaps *he* could be more valuable as a clergyman than as a doctor, just as many people are more valuable as doctors than they would be as clergymen.

When he returned home, he told his family about the turn of his thinking. The response was chilling. Immediately, they began to talk about how awful the ministry is, how low the salaries are, how difficult it woud be for his family. It was all right for other people's sons to go into the ministry, but this family had a tradition to uphold. Furthermore, medicine guaranteed a good income and a social position. But Bill persisted in his arguments. He wanted to go to college and take the pre-theological course and then go to seminary. Finally his father put the issue this way:

"If you take the premed course and go to med school, I'll finance the whole proposition, and when you're through you can share and finally inherit my practice. This will carry on the family name in medicine. But if you insist on this tomfoolery about the ministry, you'll have to pay your own way through college and seminary. I'm not buying anything as silly as that."

Bill was free to choose, but parental authority had come down hard on one side, backed by about $30,000 in cold, hard cash. Furthermore, it was clear that family relations would be badly ruptured if he chose the ministry. Bill was also puzzled because both his father and mother were active in the church, and he and his brother and sisters had always attended regularly. But to be a clergyman was not good enough.

When he talked it over with two of his friends who were

classmates, they had no hesitation in advising him, "Stick to where the money is, now and later. There's no sense," they said, "in bucking your Dad's authority and family tradition."

CONSCIENTIOUS OBJECTOR

Bill had an uncle who owned a drugstore, but he had not seen him for a long time. He remembered his uncle's story. During World War II, his uncle had become a conscientious objector, refusing to bear arms but willing to take alternative service, no matter how dangerous, as long as he was unarmed. His uncle had been an ambulance driver and as a result had studied pharmacy after the war. But the family had disowned him as a coward, and now he stayed away from family gatherings.

The struggle for a life goal, in terms of education, work, and marriage, can lead to violent struggles within the family. Sometimes, as in the case of Jesus, it can lead to a complete rift. Men and women have left their homes in order to seek their goals, they have suffered the loss of family in order to become educated, to make a vocational decision, or to take a stand on an important social or moral issue.

HOW TO CHOOSE A VOCATION

More often, your parents can assist in the decision about a vocational goal. You are fortunate if you can make a decision that is sound. If you are thinking of your future occupation in Christian terms, you will know that a Christian can work in almost any capacity, and he will find a ministry in his work. The beginning of such a decision is in terms of your aptitudes. You have certain skills, abilities, and interests that are unique with you. You have developed these as part of your education, and you can develop them more if you can obtain further education. Some of these skills, aptitudes, and interests can be applied to a variety of occupations or professions, and therefore knowledge of one's self only points toward an area of vocational choice.

But there is a second qualification, for we need to do work

that is needed. Part of this is the practical issue of finding a job or creating a job, and the other is whether there is enough money in it to make a living. Only people with independent incomes can ignore the problem of working for inadequate pay. So you need to turn your skills, aptitudes, and interests in the direction of an income-producing job that is needed by society. Some of these jobs are menial, for machines cannot take the place of some kinds of monotonous, hard work. We need garbage collectors as badly as we need doctors, but different skills are required. And there are some good-paying jobs that really are not needed at all.

This brings us to the third point, for the work we do as Christians should contribute to the welfare of society. It is at this point that you may have reservations. Is the job for which you are qualified really necessary and does it make the world better? This takes care of gangsters, prostitutes, and other occupations that are against the law. But your own Christian conscience may have to make a decision on other possibilities: airline stewardess, dancer in a "girlie" show, bartender, bus conductor, truck driver, secretary to a "rat," gas station attendant, worker in a factory, and so on. In some cases, such a job might prove repugnant on the basis of ability, need, or contribution to society. You could be against flying, dancing, liquor, driving, typing, gasoline, or automation. But all of them may provide opportunities for service and Christian relationships.

Straight thinking is necessary, and it may be that your parents can help you. If you still cannot come to a conclusion, it may be wise to wait awhile, for during college years new interests develop. But if you are almost through high school and this is the end of your formal education, as it is for so many, a choice now may be necessary. You can get help from a guidance counselor at school or from a clinic that specializes in this kind of assistance. A vocational or business school might be the next step. This decision will eliminate many job possibilities, such as teaching, that require a college education.

The Christian attitude is that almost any job can be a means of ministry, even though your own choice may prove extremely difficult. The lay person has a ministry in the world, for this is where you live your life, where it can have meaning, where battles are won or lost, where political decisions are made, where economic changes take place. These things do not happen in the family or in church. So we look to shop and store, to factory and office, to school and government office, and we see in these places the events that shape our lives.

THE MARKS OF A CHRISTIAN

An early Christian writer described the marks of a Christian:

Christians are not distinguished from the rest of mankind in country or speech or customs. For they do not live somewhere in cities of their own or use some distinctive language or practice a peculiar manner of life . . . They take part in everything like citizens, and endure everything like aliens . . . Like everyone else they marry, they have children, but they do not expose their infants. They set a common table, but not a common bed . . . They obey the established laws, and in their own lives they surpass the laws. They love all men, and are persecuted by all men . . . They are in need of all things, and they abound in all things . . . By the Jews they are warred upon as aliens, and by the Greeks they are persecuted, and those who hate them can not give a reason for their hostility. To put it briefly, what the soul is to the body, Christians are to the world.[2]

The Christian logic behind this description is peculiar. You do not start by trying to earn God's approval in the world. Because you are saved by grace through faith, *therefore* you are to be worthy of your vocation (Eph. 2:8-9; 4:1). You were initiated into this ministry through your baptism, and you need to be equipped for work in his service. You have your own unique gifts or talents, and God gave them to you. *Therefore,* you take them and develop them until they are worthy to be offered to God as you carry out your work in the world. But because all of us remain alienated to some degree, we know that we cannot be worthy. We are caught in the tension between

[2] "The Address to Diognetus," in *The Apostolic Fathers,* ed. by Edgar J. Goodspeed. New York: Harper and Brothers, 1950, p. 278.

the marks of a Christian and what we really are. The Christian, therefore, turns to God in repentance, knowing that he has been forgiven in Christ and that his alienation has been overcome by God.

In spite of the uniqueness of Jesus' ministry as the Messiah or Christ, he grew up like any other boy. He must have had an inkling of his special gifts and special responsibility when he made the trip with his parents to Jerusalem, but he was still in the process of training his gifts. There is a long period of time of which we have no record, and then at about the age of thirty he was baptized by John and knew himself called to a special ministry. He still had to struggle with the meaning of his calling, and therefore he faced his temptations over a period of forty days before it became clear to him what he would have to do. It was at this point that he began his ministry, which seemed to be highly successful in terms of teaching and healing, and yet he was opposed by his friends and family in Nazareth and had to go it alone.

What is important in this story for you is that you also will be working through to an understanding of your own gifts, will be trying to discover what training you need, and then will be spending the rest of your life working out the implications in a rapidly changing world. Your parents are likely to support you in this process, but from time to time you may expect misunderstanding and even opposition, and this is part of your trial as you seek clarity of purpose.

can we forgive our parents?

When my children were very young, as a father I am sure that I made many mistakes. During that period I discovered for the first time the following prayer-poem:

> Last night my little boy confessed to me
> Some childish wrong;
> And, kneeling at my knee
> He prayed with tears—
> "Dear God, make me a man
> Like Daddy, wise and strong;
> I know you can."
> Then, while he slept
> I knelt beside his bed,
> Confessed my sins,
> And prayed with low-bowed head,
> "O God, make me a child
> Like my child here—
> Pure, guileless,
> Trusting thee with faith sincere." [1]

YOU CAN BE A MINISTER TO YOUR PARENTS

Parents need forgiveness. Parents have a strong influence on their children in terms of being models rather than in terms of words. The child imitates Daddy's walk, his accent, his temper tantrums, his irritability, and his tricks for getting out of his

[1] By Andrew Gillies. Reprinted by permission of Mrs. John C. Leffler.

73

share of the housework. But it is always a shock to a father to see his child imitating one of his bad habits.

When children are young, they idolize their fathers. Father can do no wrong. He can be imitated without fear of reprisal. About the time the child enters kindergarten, however, he begins to see some of his father's weaknesses, but already he has been molded to be like his father. There comes a time, however, usually in early adolescence, when a father appears to be rather dumb. We are familiar with the old story of the man who looked back on his period of youth and said, "When I was fourteen my father was awfully dumb; but when I was twenty-one I was amazed at how much the old man had learned in seven years."

Because no parents are perfect, they need the strength and the power that comes from Christian faith. They need to be ministered to by those who love them. They need to be forgiven by God and reconciled to him. And in this process, nothing is more important than forgiveness by their children. Parents do not always know this, and the forgiveness by their children may be given secretly, the parents being unaware of what is happening.

THE WORLD WE LIVE IN

Much of modern literature portrays the sense of loneliness and meaninglessness. Despair and hopelessness grasp many parents as well as their children. It always seems to be too late to do anything about it. It is hopeless to commit suicide or run away. Modern writers put this insight in different ways.

You may remember Willie Loman, the father in *Death of a Salesman,* by Arthur Miller. He always had exaggerated ideas of his own importance, had always promised that some day he would be in the money, and had thought of himself as a successful father. The story is about his pitiable attempt to achieve impossible goals. Furthermore, the goals would not have solved his problem even if he had achieved them. All the despair and loneliness of his life are evident in his suicide. His son's comment, which is one of the saddest lines in literature, was, "He **never knew who he was.**"

Bishop Kilmer Myers tells of his work on the East Side of New York City in *Light the Dark Streets*. He had won the confidence of one of the gangs, called the Black Knights, and he told them that he had offered prayers both for this gang and for their sworn enemies.

"What did you offer it for *them* for?" was the natural question.

"Listen, you guys," said Myers, "Our Lord Jesus Christ took the rap for all of us. This morning we offered thanks to God for what he did when they nailed him to the cross. Understand?"

And Myers comments, "Well, they didn't. They didn't dig why Christ felt he had to take the rap for them or for anyone else." These boys had never known anyone who would take the rap for them, either parents or friends, and they had no basis for understanding why Christ had done so. Myers tried to show them what it meant by being a pastor who supported them and forgave them, and the result was a dim light which began to shine in the dark street of their lives.[2]

This frustration reaches its peak for all of us when we are not treated as persons. Take God out of the picture, and you have the feeling that anything you do will end up as meaningless. Gian Carlo Menotti, in the opera *The Consul*, tells how Magda, whose husband has fled from the country, tries to get through the red tape and obtain permission to join her husband.

> MAGDA: I must see my John, and you, only you, can help me. May I speak to the Consul?
> SECRETARY: I give you these papers, that is how to begin. Your name is a number, your story is a case, your need a request, your hopes will be filed. Come back next week.
> MAGDA: And will you explain to the Consul?
> SECRETARY: But what is there to explain?
> MAGDA: Explain that John is a hero . . . Explain that the web of my life has worn down to one single thread, that the hands of the clock glitter like knives. Explain to the Consul, explain!
> SECRETARY: But what is there to explain?
> MAGDA: Explain that John is a hero, explain that he's

2 *Light the Dark Streets*, by C. Kilmer Myers, Greenwich, Conn.: Seabury Press, 1957; Garden City: Doubleday, p. 58.

my John! Explain to the Consul, explain! Tell him my
name, tell him my story, tell him my need!
SECRETARY: Fill in these papers, that is how to begin.
Your name is a number, your story is a case, your
need a request, your hopes will be filed. Come back
next week.[3]

VICIOUS PESSIMISM

When people get angry enough about being treated as a number or a case, they are likely to flail their arms in angry poetry,
as when George Barker spells "God" in reverse and gets "dog."

Incubus. Anaesthetist with glory in a bag.
Foreman with a sweatbox and a whip.
Asphixiator
Of the ecstatic. Sergeant with a grudge
Against the lost lovers in the park of creation,
Fiend behind the fiend behind the fiend behind the
Friend. Mastodon with mastery, monster with an ache
At the tooth of the ego, the dead drunk judge:
Whoever Thou art our agony will find Thee
Enthroned on the darkest altar of our heartbreak
Perfect. Beast, brute, bastard.
O dog my God![4]

This is a vicious form of pessimism. But the point is that
when people are separated from God, when they are lonely in
the midst of people, when they are frustrated because their
dreams are not realized, they feel the agony of a terrible anxiety.
They are lost and need to be found. They are sinners in need
of redemption. They are the unloved in need of forgiving love.

You probably have never felt this way, but you may have approached it in moments of depression. And when your parents
look on their responsibilities for you, their need to provide authority, and the needless misunderstandings that result, they
need your forgiveness.

[3] *The Consul*, by G. C. Menotti, New York: © 1950 by G. Schirmer,
Inc. Used by permission.

[4] *Eros in Dogma*, by George Barker, London: Faber & Faber, 1944,
p. 37. Used by permission.

FINDING MEANING IN THE FAMILY

The Dark at the Top of the Stairs, a play by William Inge, dealt with a family that was in bad shape. There was little or no communication between the mother and the father, the children got on their parents' and their own nerves, and everything went from bad to worse. The daughter went to a ball at the country club on a blind date with a Jewish boy, who was ostracized, ignored, and cut dead and who committed suicide afterwards. It was this shock that led the family into despair, then into communication, and finally into the creation of a sounder set of relationships.

Every family has difficulties, but you need to understand family life in its wider scope if you are to be fully a responsible member of it. Think of the forces that may hold your family together:

First, there is the affection which brought your parents together, with the romantic appeal of personal attraction, the enjoyment of each other, and the desire for permanence. The fire may die down, but there is warmth in the embers that continues through life.

Second, your parents began married life with a responsible decision. They gave their free consent to what was intended to be a lifelong relationship. The permanence of their decision was the crucial point.

Third, even before you came along, your mother and father had become a team. They made many decisions about you jointly, whenever it was possible, and as you grew older you were drawn into some of the family decisions.

Fourth, we are all creatures of habit. Mother and father and children tend to take each other for granted. Family traditions remain unchanged.

Behind these forces which tend to keep a family together and to restore relationships that have been broken, is the power of the Holy Spirit. The gift of love in marriage ultimately comes from God. The Holy Spirit is like the *esprit de corps,* the morale which holds a school or church or family together. He is the source of healing power by which God reconciles men to each other.

Your family, then, can become a redemptive community, in which the love of God is at work through forgiveness, love, and restoration. All of you have a ministry to each of the others.

DO YOU FORGIVE YOUR PARENTS?

You have probably forgiven your parents secretly many times, not in words but in actions. They have forgiven you even more often. Usually forgiveness seems good. It puts a child back in his mother's arms, where he knows by physical contact that he is loved, and where she knows by the same token that she is loved.

But when you have gone to your room and locked yourself in, and want to have nothing to do with your mother or father because you think they have been unfair, all they can do is wait. You have control of the situation. You can stay there as long as you want; you can come out and be nasty and unapproachable, and eat your meal in silence; you can resolve that you will keep everything to yourself from now on, especially if what you said got you into trouble. You'll show them.

Your parents will be miserably unhappy. They probably are not sure why you are upset, but if they know, they wonder what they could have done differently. You may have been unreasonable, or perhaps you did not have a chance to explain or you would not listen, so there was no communication. The single word "No!" followed by the banging of a door is not exactly an intelligent conversation.

If you have thought things through and decided that you **would** like to patch things up, it is not difficult to do in most **cases** (unless your parents are childish, too). You do not need to say "I'm sorry," or "Forgive me," or "I forgive you." You usually do not need to say anything. You reappear with an attitude that communicates how you feel. If clarification is needed, you can try to open up some channels for listening and speaking "the truth in love."

Occasionally you will get stuck with parents who will not

admit being wrong. Therefore, they are not open to forgiveness, and this will provide a short-circuit of the line back to them and to God. All that is left is your willingness to forgive, and to wait until they are enabled to receive it. This requires fortitude, steadfastness, and further hurt. But it is what Jesus meant by saying we should forgive "until seventy times seven."

FORGIVENESS AND GOD

Forgiveness goes back to God. We hear the stories of two lost sons. The first was the Prodigal, who wasted his money in riotous living and ended up in a pigpen, hungry and dirty and miserable. In this condition, he "came to himself" and saw what an ass he had made of himself. He contrasted his condition with that of his father's servants and decided that he would be much better off if his father would let him join them. He knew he had no right to ask to be restored as a son.

So he headed for home and his father spotted him from a distance and ran to greet him. The son was repentant and told his father so, and could he be a servant for his father? And his father said that he would not be a servant but a son. His father turned to his servants and said, "Quick! fetch a robe, my best one, and put it on him; put a ring on his finger and shoes on his feet. Bring the fatted calf and kill it, and let us have a feast to celebrate this day. For this son of mine was dead and has come back to life; he was lost and is found." (Lk. 15:22-24, NEB.)

When the older brother, the good boy who never did anything wrong, heard music and dancing as he approached the house, he wanted to know what had happened. He became angry and refused to go in. His father came out and pleaded with him, but he answered, "You know how I have slaved for you all these years; I never once disobeyed your orders; and you never gave me so much as a kid, for a feast with my friends. But now that this son of yours turns up, after running through your money with his women, you kill the fatted calf for him." (Lk. 15:29-30, NEB.)

The younger son, who finally came to accurate knowledge of

himself and his condition of separation from his father, was joyfully received as a son. The outgoing love of the father is possible for earthly fathers, but the parable points to God's forgiving love and joy that a son has returned to the fold.

The elder son is more difficult to analyze. There are Christians who believe he got a raw deal. After all, he was good, he probably never missed a Sabbath at the synagogue, and he never wandered from the farm. He was respectable, and he could not imagine himself in the company with this other son, whom he called "this son of *yours*." He did not admit him as a brother. He could not rejoice and join the dancing and feasting.

We begin to see in this story what God wants of us. We are justified by faith, which means that we cannot earn God's approval by being good. We are to trust God, and he will give us of his love. Because we are saved by faith through grace, we seek to be worthy of our calling. But we know that God is forgiving, for we know what he has done in Jesus Christ.

HOW THE CHURCH HELPS

When you go to church, you are there to worship God, to hear his Word, and to be open to the Spirit. In this worship, there are always the notes of confession, when you have the opportunity to "come to yourself"; absolution, when you hear that God forgives you and restores you to sonship; hearing, when you hear Scripture and the sermon, and through them you become aware of God's claim on your life; affirmation, when you recite the creed or some other symbol of your loyalty; petition, when you pray for your sincere desires; intercession, when you pray for others; thanksgiving, when among other things you thank God for the gift of Jesus Christ; and benediction, when you hear God's blessing pronounced. Mixed in with all this are hymns expressing all of these attitudes. The Lord's Supper reminds us that Christ is present in our total personalities through faith.

In one sense, this experience takes a load off our shoulders. We hear Jesus Christ say; "Come unto me, all of you who toil and are burdened" (G), or "that labor and are heavy laden"

(KJ), or "that travail" (PB)—"And I will refresh you" (PB), or "I will give you rest" (KJ).

"Let my yoke be put on you, and learn from me, for I am gentle and humble-minded, and your hearts will find rest, for the yoke I offer you is a kindly one, and the load I ask you to bear is light" (Mt. 11:28-30, G).

Perhaps the best way for you to forgive your parents is to pray for them. There are two prayers which are extremely helpful:

"O God, whose fatherly care reacheth to the uttermost parts of the earth; We humbly beseech thee graciously to behold and bless those whom we love. Defend them from all dangers of soul and body; and grant that both they and we, drawing nearer to thee, may be bound together by thy love in the communion of thy Holy Spirit, and in the fellowship of thy saints; through Jesus Christ our Lord. Amen."

"Almighty God, we entrust all who are dear to us to thy never-failing care and love, for this life and the life to come; knowing that thou art doing for them better things than we can desire or pray for; through Jesus Christ our Lord. Amen."

These are the prayers of the mature Christian, and they may open the way for God to help you achieve reconciliation with your parents. You *can* forgive your parents; and they can forgive you.

open
channels
of
communication

Some people are cynical about marriage, as was Jerome (the translator of the Latin Bible), who said, "I do not condemn wedlock. Indeed . . . I should like everyone to take a wife who cannot manage to sleep alone because he gets frightened at night." But the church has taught that marriage is good.

Your family may no longer be a unity: one parent may be dead, your parents may be separated or divorced, one parent may belong to another church or none. But I am thinking of you as a church member who has one parent at least who is also a church member. To this extent, at least, you and your family are a unity under the lordship of Christ. You can think of your family as a cell of the larger body of Christ, the Church.

When a family thinks of itself as a Christian family, it sees its fellowship in a new light. The Greek word is *koinonia*, which means community, communion, fellowship, participation, or sharing. Members of a Christian family are a community; they try to stay in communion with each other; they experience a level of fellowship which is especially meaningful; they participate in the ministry of Christians; and they share in the gifts which God has given them.

No family achieves this kind of community, because the members are far from perfect. Yet every Christian family has some experiences which meet this description. It may be at a moment of celebration, at Christmas or on a birthday; it may be when one member has achieved something of importance, as at a graduation; it may be in a moment of crisis, when one member is in deep trouble; it may be in a moment of tragedy, when the whole family is drawn together by accident or death. The natural connections of family relationships are very strong, even when there are forces pulling apart the various members.

SOME GOALS TO WORK FOR

Some families are aware of these resources and seek to provide conditions where each member will have a strong sense of security within the family. The children and adolescents in the family, who sometimes feel isolated from genuine communication with their parents, may help to set up helpful conditions. The parents, knowing that family solidarity must be worked for, may take the lead. Marjorie Reeves, in a little book called *Growing Up in a Modern Society,*[1] writes that such a community must meet five conditions:

1. In each family "the life of the group must be subject to the rule of a law which is beneficent and consistent and—as far as possible—willingly accepted by each member." These laws, as has been shown, have to be altered as the children grow older, but laws provide a way of life for the whole family.

2. The members of the family "must treat each other as persons." It is clear that this means that each member is an end in himself. No one is to use another member as a "thing" in order to get what he wants. The welfare of each member as a person should be the concern of all the others.

3. "Each member must find a significant role to play in the life of the whole, the purpose of which he understands as fully as possible." The family that works together, plays together, and prays together is likely to stay together. But this means that the members of the family must take the time to be in the presence of the others long enough to establish "significant roles."

4. There must be "mixture" in the family, so that there

[1] University of London Press, 1946, p. 35.

are "tensions and differences to be experienced." When the atmosphere is such that persons are free to be themselves there will be differences of opinion, freedom of discussion, and sometimes conflict as to what activities will be followed. This is healthy as long as the other conditions are being met.

5. The family "must serve some purpose bigger than the immediate self-interest of its members." This is the Christian note in family life. The members have a sense of *koinonia* because the Holy Spirit is at work in their midst. But this communion, if it becomes ingrown, can be destroyed. Members of a family must not only serve each other, but they also have a ministry to their neighbors, to social causes, to activities in the neighborhood and in the church.

These goals are not easily achieved. Parents are not always aware that these conditions are essential to family life at its best. Communication is not always possible. But there are certain things that you can do to keep open the channels of communication. The most important thing you can do is to understand what communication is. You are likely to be so concerned to get *your* point across that you do not listen to what your parents say; and they are still caught in the image of the all-wise parent and do not listen to you before they give forth words of wisdom.

DIALOGUE

The key word is "dialogue." This means that two people are involved in both talking and listening. It is a two-way communication system. It has been described as "that address and response between persons in which there is a flow of meaning between them in spite of all the obstacles that would normally block the relationship." [2]

Let us look at this definition and see where the difficulties lie, for you are the one who can do something about this. Dialogue involves "address and response." You not only speak, but you listen. As you listen, you respond to what has been said. This enables the other to understand that you are responding to him,

[2] *The Miracle of Dialogue,* by Reuel L. Howe, New York: Seabury Press, 1963, p. 37.

and therefore he listens to you. This leads to a "flow of meaning" back and forth. He begins to see what you are driving at, and therefore he speaks to your situation. But of course there are "obstacles."

Sally put it this way: "I have a swell mother. She listens to what I say. But then she puts me right, and that's all there is to it. All I get is a monologue."

This is a standard problem. Many young people believe that their parents do not want to give the time to listen to them. Sally would like to tell her mother what is going on, and then discuss the issues with her, but her mother likes to speak with authority, and then the conversation is not only ended but is dead.

Some families find that the dinner hour provides an opportunity for discussion of all sorts of things. Personal problems may not provide the best topic for dinner conversations, but many interests at school, in the sports world, in politics, and in other activities help to build up a sense of community. In these areas, parents are more likely to participate in the give and take of a variety of opinions, and they come to respect the judgment of their children.

MUTUAL INVOLVEMENT

Another factor in communication is mutual involvement. When parents and their young people become engaged in a common activity, this helps provide a basis for conversation. Families that go to church together, have a picnic, join a work project in the back yard, or travel, find that they have much in common to talk about. Boys frequently engage their fathers in sharing their hobbies. Girls find activities they can share with their mothers. Such mutual interests and activities build a basis for dialogue.

The Smith family attended a church which had a family worship service. This was something special at 9:15, in which everything that happened in their worship was intended for parents, young people, and children. The hymns and lessons were carefully selected to meet the needs of a specialized group.

The service lasted about thirty-five to forty minutes. The sermon was geared to the kinds of experience common to family members in the congregation. The Bible was interpreted in terms which helped everyone present think about its meaning. The parents had classes afterwards at the same time as the children.

When the Smith family got in the station wagon for the ride home, all the members had shared a common experience of worship about which they could talk intelligently. Father and mother, as well as the boys and girls, had questions to ask, interpretations to make, and further studying to do in order to see more clearly what meaning the worship had for them. This became a chief topic at the Sunday dinner table.

COMMUNICATION AND RELATIONSHIPS

Good communication creates relationships. When it is possible to talk things through, so that genuine dialogue occurs, members of a family can afford to differ on important issues and yet respect the opinions of the others.

Bob and his father had a long argument about the use of the family car. Bob thought he ought to be able to use it to drive to school. His father had good reasons why this should not be allowed. Bob put up all kinds of arguments, chiefly in terms of friends he knew who drove to school, and he called his father a "skinflint." His father was able to reflect Bob's feelings: "Yes Bob, I know you think I'm being mean, and I agree that you have a right to feel that way, but in this case I have to make the final decision, which is 'No.' " Bob did not like it, but he knew that his father knew how he felt, and therefore their relationship remained healthy. But if Bob's father had simply said, "I don't give a darn how you feel and what I say is final, so shut up," Bob would have felt rejected by his father and their relationship would have been strained.

Good relationships also make possible communication. If you *know* your parents love you because of your relationships over the years, their moments of anger or injustice or shortsightedness can be taken in stride. Jack's father drank too much on occasion. He sometimes went down into the basement room and got drunk, and then he became remorseful and threatened to kill himself. Jack came down with a tray of food and his father began to cry. Jack assured him that he loved him, that the whole family loved him. And his father dried his tears, went to sleep, and woke up sober but with a hangover. His father returned upstairs the next day, and his family received him as if nothing unusual had occurred. They accepted him as he was, in spite of his weakness for drink, and their mutual love supported this relationship through the years.

If you have been fortunate, you and your parents have kept open the channels of communication. When they seemed to be closed, you or they have found ways to reopen the dialogue, so that there was a two-way communication between you. This exchange of meanings made possible your growth and development toward a goal for your life. And as you have approached maturity, you have relied less and less on their authority, but you have not cut off the possibility of genuine dialogue.

WHEN FAMILIES BREAK UP

Families do break up. Divorce rates run about 6 per cent when both parents share the same faith, and they run much higher when there are differences about religion or when there is no church affiliation. In some situations, family relations become so strained that it is impossible for a father and mother to live in the same house. Separation without divorce is sometimes tried, but usually the result is divorce. Furthermore, in many cases, one or the other marries someone else.

Whenever there is a family separation, it is hard on both the children and the parents. The mother usually is given custody of the children, and the father may have visiting rights. Sometimes the father has the children for part of the year or even complete custody. On rare occasions, the father or mother does not see the children at all. Remarriage leads to a stepfather or stepmother.

The situation is always complicated, especially in terms of emotional ties. When there is continued bitterness between the father and mother, the children sometimes take sides. But usually the children are drawn to both parents after the divorce, and they try to be neutral when there are further disputes. Older children and young people, who understand the situation, usually attempt to keep open the channels of communication between themselves and both parents.

Young people also are capable of seeing what happens to a divorced mother who has to fill the role of a father as well. When there is no uncle or male friend to call upon, the growing children do not have the experience of a man in the house. This results in an emotional blind spot for the children that may affect their future relationships with men. Mothers try to fill this gap in various ways, either by encouraging the divorced father to see more of his children, or by providing opportunities for the children to know other men, or by remarriage.

A similar sense of emotional loss is experienced when a father dies. In this case there is no tension or conflict due to incompatibility, but the widowed mother has a similar role to fill and needs help from men to provide male companionship for her children. An oldest boy sometimes moves into this father role very successfully if he is sensitive to the needs of his brothers and sisters.

These breaks in family life make a difference to children of all ages, and they cannot do much to help, except as a mother or father who is left communicates to them the meaning of what is happening. Everything is brought out into the open for understanding. This draws the children even closer to the remaining parent and can prove to be a very healthy situation.

IMPORTANT QUESTIONS

As you discover the means of keeping open the lines of communication with your parents (and each of you will find your own ways of achieving dialogue and avoiding parental monologues), you will discover that important questions come to mind. Instead of discussing late hours, study habits, money problems, your friends, and your education, you will begin to find that you and your parents have ideas of what you should do with your life.

Some of you girls are already thinking of marriage, but if you are realistic you may find that it is equally important to think about a job. If you are thinking about both marriage and a job, you are thinking about the preparation for them in terms of further education or vocational training. You may be asking these questions in terms of getting along in the world, finding the right man, and obtaining a job you like that pays enough. These are important questions and your parents can be helpful in discussions as you evaluate yourself and your opportunities.

Some of you boys are thinking in terms of an area of work, with marriage in the background for future consideration. You may have chosen your father as an example and want to follow his career, or your father may want you to join his business and you may not be interested. This is a difficult matter to talk through because your father has invested so much of himself in his work over the years. A boy who is a natural salesman would be unhappy as a teacher, and a boy with musical interests would hate clerking in his father's furniture store. Your parents can sometimes help you to see clearly what your aptitudes are, but in other cases you and your parents may need help from a vocational counselor. It is not easy, especially in the complexity of today's technical society, to make a decision about work and the proper preparation for it.

But your life is not restricted to marriage or work. The key question is, What can I do with my *life?* What meaning am I going to find in all that I do with everything that I have? Every person has a unique set of aptitudes. Some of you are familiar with the biblical way of putting it. The Letter to the Ephesians put it this way: "And these were his gifts: some to be apostles, some prophets, some evangelists, some pastors and teachers, to equip God's people for work in his service, to the building up of the body of Christ" (Eph. 4:11-12, NEB). The key to this passage is that we all have specific *gifts,* and as Christians we are to be *equipped* for work in his service. The answer to the question, What can I do with my life? is that we are to take the gifts of our individual personalities and have them equipped so that they can be used in the service of God and man. Your life itself is a gift, and as you grow to maturity you learn how best to use this gift. "We are no longer to be children, tossed by the waves and whirled about by every fresh gust of teaching, dupes of crafty rogues and their deceitful schemes. No, let us speak the truth in love; so shall we fully grow up in Christ" (Eph. 4:14-15, NEB). We have to travel the rocky road of adolescence before we can get to the point at which we are no longer tossed to and fro by all sorts of enthusiasms.

As you move out of the orbit of parental authority and become your own boss, you have to live in the world. This world includes new authorities, new people, new pressures. You can continue to grow or you can suffer from arrested development. You can build on what you are now, or you can stop building and start drifting.

MATURITY

Your goal is Christian maturity. Some people never reach it. Your parents are not consistently mature. How you have handled yourself in relationship to your parents is your foundation. But as you begin to see clearly what it means to be "measured by nothing less than the full stature of Christ," you are moving toward maturity.

Reuel L. Howe describes maturity in the following statements:

> We are mature to the extent that we are guided by our long-term purposes rather than by our immediate desires.
> The mature person is able to accept things and people the way they are, rather than pretend they are the way he wants them to be.
> The mature person is able to accept the authority of others without the rebellion or without the self-abdication that we call "folding up."
> The mature person is one who is able to accept himself as an authority without either a sense of bravado or a sense of guilt.
> A mature person is able to defend himself both from his own unacceptable impulses and from attacks from the outside.
> The mature person is able to work without being a

slave, and to play without feeling that he ought to be working.

A mature person is one who is able to accept his own, and the opposite, sex and the relation between the two in ways that are appropriately fulfilling.

The mature person is one who is able to love others so satisfyingly that he becomes less dependent on being loved.

Finally, the mature person is one who is able to accept his significant place and role in the larger scheme of things.[3]

As you grow toward maturity you will become the kind of person who can do these things. You will have moments of doubt, of failure, of being separated from other people and from God. But you will also develop an attitude of basic trust, because you have been exposed not only to life in the church (which is sometimes disappointing) but also to the hope for all men described in the Christian gospel. You will think about the meaning of your life in words and ideas that are different from those of your parents, teachers, and pastors, and often from those of your friends.

The Christian finds his faith primarily in the Bible, which is a record of what God has done through a small group of people. It helps you to understand what it means to be a creature who is limited in space and time and who is related to a Creator who is eternal. It helps you to understand what it is to be responsible, to keep an agreement, to be a member of a community under the claims of God. It helps you when you are lonely or anxious or alienated, when you have a sense of guilt because you have failed as a responsible person, for the good news is that "God was in Christ reconciling the world to himself" (2 Cor. 5:19, NEB). You can be forgiven and restored to a proper relationship with God and your fellows. You may have learned some of this from your parents, but chiefly you and they learned this in the church. Because you have been led to trust the God who has given you the gift of life, you are enabled to live today so that you will not be afraid to die.

[3] *The Creative Years*, by Reuel L. Howe, New York: Seabury Press, 1965, pp. 198-208.

JUSTIFIED BY FAITH

God knows what shape you are in. He knows that you have trouble being honest, even with yourself. He knows that you do not meet your side of the agreement, of his hope for your obedience to him. If you had to take a test on your knowledge, your trust, or your behavior, you think that you would flunk.

Because God is God, he has moved in on you, whether you know it or not. He made this clear when he acted through Jesus Christ, a man whose victory over death was also a victory over spiritual deadness. This is the start of real life, real freedom, real power, real love for all who trust him.

St. Paul called this "justification by faith." All you have to do is to accept the fact that God accepts you as you are, and this is not easy. But the results are exciting. You are not saved through anything that you do, for all you can do is to trust a God who comes alive in our midst. You do not see him, and yet you respond to the mystery of his seeking and forgiving love. *Therefore,* because of what God has done, you are to serve him in your daily life.

Grace means God in action—his free gift of himself and his love. Faith means your response—your decision, commitment, and trust in him. This is the odd logic of the gospel. Because of what God has done, you are to do much. You have a ministry because you were baptized into it. The church is called the body of Christ, and you are a member, just as a finger or an eye is a member of your body; and you are to function as a Christian in the world.

Your parents have had the obligation to assist in equipping you for this ministry, even though they may not have realized it. They have worked at their ministry of teaching, sometimes effectively and sometimes not. They may have abdicated their task and left everything to the church. But in so far as they have taken *their* ministry as parents seriously, they have been concerned about you. And now that you are moving toward maturity, you will need to continue learning how to use your gifts in the service of your Lord.

There is a great hymn by F. Bland Tucker which summarizes some of these insights:

> Our Father, by whose Name
> All fatherhood is known,
> Who dost in love proclaim
> Each family thine own,
> Bless thou all parents, guarding well,
> With constant love as sentinel,
> The homes in which thy people dwell.

> O Christ, thyself a child
> Within an earthly home,
> With heart still undefiled,
> Thou didst to manhood come;
> Our children bless, in every place,
> That they may all behold thy face,
> And knowing thee may grow in grace.

> O Spirit, who dost bind
> Our hearts in unity,
> Who teachest us to find
> The love from self set free,
> In all our hearts such love increase,
> That every home, by this release,
> May be the dwelling place of peace.[4]

[4] F. Bland Tucker, *The Hymnal 1940*, New York: Church Pension Fund, 1943, No. 504. By permission of The Church Pension Fund.